*Winston Churchill*

# VIP
*Very Interesting People*

*Bite-sized biographies of Britain's most fascinating historical figures*

| | |
|---|---|
| 1. **William Shakespeare** | *Peter Holland* |
| 2. **George Eliot** | *Rosemary Ashton* |
| 3. **Charles Dickens** | *Michael Slater* |
| 4. **Charles Darwin** | *Adrian Desmond, James Moore, and Janet Browne* |
| 5. **Isaac Newton** | *Richard S. Westfall* |
| 6. **Elizabeth I** | *Patrick Collinson* |
| 7. **George III** | *John Cannon* |
| 8. **Benjamin Disraeli** | *Jonathan Parry* |
| 9. **Christopher Wren** | *Kerry Downes* |
| 10. **John Ruskin** | *Robert Hewison* |
| 11. **James Joyce** | *Bruce Stewart* |
| 12. **John Milton** | *Gordon Campbell* |
| 13. **Jane Austen** | *Marilyn Butler* |
| 14. **Henry VIII** | *Eric Ives* |
| 15. **Queen Victoria** | *K. D. Reynolds and H. C. G. Matthew* |
| 16. **Winston Churchill** | *Paul Addison* |
| 17. **Oliver Cromwell** | *John Morrill* |
| 18. **Thomas Paine** | *Mark Philp* |
| 19. **J. M. W. Turner** | *Luke Herrmann* |
| 20. **William and Mary** | *Tony Claydon and W. A. Speck* |

# *Winston Churchill*

VIP
*Very Interesting People*

Paul Addison

OXFORD
UNIVERSITY PRESS

**OXFORD**
UNIVERSITY PRESS

Great Clarendon Street, Oxford OX2 6DP

Oxford University Press is a department of the University of Oxford.
It furthers the University's objective of excellence in research, scholarship,
and education by publishing worldwide in

Oxford New York

Auckland Cape Town Dar es Salaam Hong Kong Karachi
Kuala Lumpur Madrid Melbourne Mexico City Nairobi
New Delhi Shanghai Taipei Toronto

With offices in

Argentina Austria Brazil Chile Czech Republic France Greece
Guatemala Hungary Italy Japan Poland Portugal Singapore
South Korea Switzerland Thailand Turkey Ukraine Vietnam



Published in the United States
by Oxford University Press Inc., New York

First published in the *Oxford Dictionary of National Biography* 2004
This paperback edition first published 2007



First published 2007



British Library Cataloguing in Publication Data

Data available

Library of Congress Cataloging in Publication Data

Data available

Typeset by SPI Publisher Services, Pondicherry, India
Printed in Great Britain
on acid-free paper by
Clays Ltd, St Ives plc

ISBN 978-0-19-953456-2

1

# Contents

# *Preface*

I hope this short biography, originally written for the *Oxford Dictionary of National Biography*, will be of particular use to readers in search of a concise introduction to a long and complex subject. My own curiosity about Churchill dates back to the distant era when I first embarked on historical research. It was 1964 and my field was Britain in the Second World War. I had beside me the six volumes of Churchill's war memoirs, but looking back I am astonished to realize how little I knew of the rest of his life. I was fortunate in my supervisor, A. J. P. Taylor, a wonderful historian whose conversation had the magical effect of making the past more real than the present. His insights were all the more valuable because of the dearth of material in print. Research into the history of twentieth-century Britain had scarcely begun and a fifty-year rule restricted the release of official documents. Churchill himself was still alive and the contents of his papers a closely guarded secret.

Then suddenly the picture changed. In January 1965 Churchill died. Tongues were loosened and a debate opened up which has continued, in one form of another, ever since. The fifty-year rule was replaced by a thirty-year rule. One by one there began to appear the mighty volumes of the official biography. In the decades that followed I kept a watching brief on the many controversies that ensued and witnessed the literature on Churchill grow from a trickle into a torrent. I myself wrote about his religious and political beliefs, his role in home affairs, and what might rather grandly be called 'the historiography of Churchill.' This could be more accurately described as a kaleidoscope of opinions in which the clearest dividing line was between those who maintained that Churchill was the saviour of his country in the Second World War and those who argued that for most practical purposes he led Britain to defeat.

Historians still differ, but much of the heat has gone from the debate, and light may be taking its place. Underlying all the arguments about the merits of Churchill's judgement on this or that occasion is a question about his nature as a political animal. I often found this a difficult problem. His private life, though not always happy, was remarkably straightforward. His public life was full of contradictions and seemed to be the work of a number of different people. Eventually I grasped the simple fact that, up to a point, it was. I had been trying to construct Churchill as a fixed character pursuing a linear path. He was in fact a restless, intuitive force who re-invented himself at frequent intervals and hardly knew where imagination and opportunity would carry him next. True, he always remained a late Victorian imperialist, a soldier, and a Tory Democrat at heart, but these were broad conceptions like the 'sunlit uplands' to which he sometimes alluded. With Churchill we always have to remember that he was writing his own script and making up the story as he went along.

*Paul Addison*
*February 2007*



## *About the author*

Paul Addison is the author of *The Road to 1945: British Politics and the Second World War* (1975), *Churchill on the Home Front, 1900–1955* (1992), and *Churchill: the Unexpected Hero* (2005). He is an Honorary Fellow in the School of History and Classics at the University of Edinburgh, where he was Director of the Centre for Second World War Studies from 1996 to 2005.

# Youthful adventures

# 1

*Sir Winston Leonard Spencer Churchill* (1874–1965), prime minister, was born at Blenheim Palace, Oxfordshire, the family home of the dukes of Marlborough, on 30 November 1874. His father, Lord Randolph Henry Spencer Churchill (1849–1895), was the third son of the seventh duke and a descendant of John Churchill, first duke of Marlborough, Queen Anne's commander-in-chief during the War of the Spanish Succession. His mother, Jeanette (Jennie) Churchill (1854–1921), was the daughter of Leonard Jerome, a New York financier whose ancestors had fought against the British in the American War of Independence. According to a Jerome family tradition accepted by Churchill himself, Jennie's mother, Clara, was of Iroquois descent, but proof is lacking.

## Schooldays: flouting the rules

Jennie and Lord Randolph were married at the British embassy in Paris on 15 April 1874. Winston Churchill's date of birth has given rise to speculation that he was conceived before the wedding, but the only certainty is that he was born prematurely. Preparations were made for the birth to take place in London, but after slipping and falling during a visit to Blenheim Jennie went into labour, the local doctor was summoned, and the baby was delivered at 1.30 a.m. on 30 November.

When the seventh duke was appointed viceroy of Ireland in January 1877, the Churchills moved to Dublin. Winston was accompanied by his nanny, Mrs Elizabeth Everest, who took him for walks in Phoenix Park and warned him against a group of evil men known as Fenians. Shortly after the birth of his brother John Strange Spencer (Jack) Churchill (1880–1947) in February 1880, the family returned to London, where Winston began to build up an impressive collection of toy soldiers in the nursery. At eight he was sent to a boarding-school at Ascot where the headmaster took a pleasure in flogging the boys until their bottoms ran with blood. Winston performed well in some subjects but his reports often referred to his unruly behaviour. According to one authority, he was birched for stealing sugar from the pantry and retaliated by kicking the headmaster's straw hat to pieces (Churchill and Gilbert, 1.53). When he fell ill his parents transferred him to a school at Brighton where he was much happier but came bottom of the class for conduct.

Neither of Churchill's parents lacked affection for Winston, but they gave him little attention and he felt profoundly neglected. Lord Randolph's short and troubled life was devoted mainly to politics: Winston could recall only two or three long and intimate conversations with him. Lady Randolph, meanwhile, revelled in high society. 'She shone for me like the Evening Star', Churchill wrote. 'I loved her dearly—but at a distance' (Churchill, *Early Life*, 19). Unlike his brother, Winston developed a powerful ego. His letters home from boarding-school were full of demands for attention, and protests against his parents' failure to meet his wishes. He was fortunate to discover in Mrs Everest a surrogate parent who gave him the love and admiration he craved. He responded with remarkably open displays of affection for his 'Woom' or 'Woomany'. Inviting her to Harrow, he showed her around the school and walked arm in arm with her up the High Street while other boys jeered at him. During her final illness in July 1895 Churchill, by this time a Sandhurst cadet, rushed to her bedside, afterwards arranging the funeral and the erection of a headstone on her grave. In his novel *Savrola* (1900) he brought her to life again as the hero's faithful housekeeper, Bettine.

Churchill entered Harrow in April 1888. Convinced that his son was not clever enough for university, Lord Randolph was impressed by the enthusiasm with which he manoeuvred his army of toy soldiers; he arranged for him to enter the army class, which prepared boys for Sandhurst. Legend has it that Winston was academically a bit of a dunce, but he demonstrated great ability in English, history, and chemistry, subjects that captured his imagination. Mathematics, however, baffled him and in spite of personal tuition from the headmaster, J. E. C. Welldon, he detested Latin. Like Richmal Crompton's fictional hero William, whom in many ways he resembled, the schoolboy Winston was a courageous individualist who flouted the rules and got into scrapes. He lacked self-discipline and his teachers often complained of slovenly or unruly behaviour, but censure or punishment served only to provoke him into a long and indignant defence of his actions. Inevitably, perhaps, team sports held little appeal for him, but in spite of frequent bouts of ill health he was a strong swimmer, excelled at rifle shooting, and won the public schools fencing championship in 1892. None of this could appease his father's wrath when he twice failed the entrance exams for Sandhurst, passing in at the third attempt with marks too low to qualify him for the infantry. Lord Randolph's response was a remarkably cruel letter in which he threatened to break off all contact with his son and warned: 'if you cannot prevent yourself from leading the idle useless unprofitable life you have had during your schooldays & later months you will become a mere social wastrel, one of the hundreds of the public school failures' (Churchill and Gilbert, 1.197).

## Cavalry officer: making a reputation

At Sandhurst, which he entered as an infantry cadet in September 1893, Churchill enjoyed himself. Military topics such as tactics or fortifications were far more appealing to him than mathematics, and horsemanship the greatest of pleasures. In high spirits and working hard, he eventually passed out twentieth out of 130. During his final term he also plunged, for the first time, into public controversy. When the eminent moral reformer Mrs Ormiston Chant organized a campaign to exclude prostitutes from the bar of the Empire Theatre in Leicester Square, Churchill incited some of his fellow cadets to riot and pull down the screens which had been put up to separate prostitutes from theatregoers. 'Ladies of the Empire', Churchill declared in an impromptu speech, 'I stand for Liberty!' (Gilbert, *Life*, 46–7).

Churchill's late adolescence was overshadowed by the physical and mental decline of Lord Randolph, who had risen to be chancellor of the exchequer in Lord Salisbury's government of 1886, but overplayed his hand, resigned, and never held office again. As a gentleman cadet Churchill had begun to win his father's respect, but just as the relationship between father and son was about to ripen it was cut short by Lord Randolph's death, at the age of forty-five, on 24 January 1895. His neurologist, Dr Buzzard, diagnosed his illness as syphilis, though it has recently been argued that his symptoms could have been caused by a tumour on the brain (Mather, 23–8).

Although unaware of Buzzard's diagnosis, Churchill believed that Lord Randolph's death, like that of his brother the eighth duke of Marlborough, 'was yet further proof that the Churchills died young' (Gilbert, *Life*, 49). Driven by the need to appease his father's ghost and vindicate his reputation, he was desperate to make his mark before it was too late. But he was also free at last of Lord Randolph's restraining hand and ready to embark on adventures of his own. After passing out from Sandhurst he obtained his commission (20 February 1895) as a cavalry officer in the 4th (Queen's Own) hussars. Here he acquired a passion for polo, a game he was to enjoy playing for the next three decades. But much as he enjoyed soldiering he regarded it as a means to an end: the making of a reputation that would propel him into the House of Commons. In October 1895 he travelled with his friend Reggie Barnes to Cuba to report on the rebellion against Spanish rule for the *Daily Graphic*. Visiting New York *en route* he was entertained by the Irish-American politician Bourke Cockran, an old flame of Lady Randolph, whose eloquence and oratory made a lasting impression on him. Churchill's twenty-first birthday (30 November 1895) found him in the company of Spanish forces suppressing a rebellion in Cuba. Here he saw shots fired in anger for the first time, and acquired two lifelong habits: Havana cigars and siestas.

In October 1896 Churchill sailed with his regiment to India. Comfortably quartered in the British military compound at Bangalore, he displayed little interest in the subcontinent around him, but followed the political news from home with the eagerness and frustration of an exile. With his thoughts fixed firmly on a parliamentary career, he was worried by the fact that unlike so many other ambitious young men he lacked a university education. Enlisting the aid of Lady Randolph, he pursued a remarkable programme of self-education. During the long afternoons while the regiment rested, he devoured the works of Plato, Adam Smith, Edward Gibbon, Thomas Babington Macaulay, Henry Hallam, Edward Lecky, Charles Darwin, and William Winwood Reade, supplemented by volumes of the *Annual Register*, in which he annotated the summaries of old parliamentary debates with imaginary contributions of his own. Churchill's reading affected both his prose style, which he modelled on Gibbon and Macaulay, and his view of the world. Winwood Reade's *Martyrdom of Man*, a classic of Victorian atheism, completed his loss of faith in orthodox Christianity and left him with a sombre vision of a godless universe in which humanity was destined, nevertheless, to progress through the conflict between the more advanced and the more backward races. He passed for a time through an aggressively anti-religious phase, but this eventually gave way to a more tolerant belief in the workings of some kind of divine providence.

Churchill's belief that he was destined to accomplish great things was accompanied by a daring scheme of self-advertisement. He told Lady Randolph:

> A few months in South Africa would earn me the S.A. medal and in all probability the Company's star. Thence hot-foot to Egypt—to return with two more decorations in a year or two—and beat my sword into an iron despatch box. (Churchill and Gilbert, *Companion*, vol. 1, pt 2, p. 676)

Between 1897 and 1900, with the aid of assiduous lobbying by his mother, he managed to fight in three of Queen Victoria's wars while doubling as a war correspondent and turning all three of his experiences into books.

## War correspondent

When the attacks of Afghan tribesmen on the north-west frontier of India led to the formation of a punitive expeditionary force, under the command of Sir Bindon Blood, Churchill obtained an attachment to the force and a contract as a war correspondent with the *Daily Telegraph*. He took part in several skirmishes in which he came under fire and witnessed acts of barbarism by both sides. On his return to Bangalore he expanded his reports into his first book, *The Story of the Malakand Field Force* (1898), which combined an incisive narrative of the fighting with vivid accounts of the landscape and its inhabitants. By this time he was also writing a novel, *Savrola*, a melodramatic tale of a liberal revolution in an autocratic Mediterranean state: the hero, Savrola, was a compound of himself and Lord Randolph. His work on the book was interrupted, in the summer of 1898, by the final stages of the campaign for the reconquest of the Sudan.

This time it was the *Morning Post* which commissioned Churchill to report the war. Overcoming the objections of Horatio Kitchener, the commander-in-chief of the expeditionary force, Churchill obtained a temporary posting with the 21st lancers, and arrived in the Sudan in time to take part in the celebrated cavalry charge at the battle of Omdurman (2 September 1898) in which the regiment galloped by accident into a hidden ravine crammed with armed men. Churchill, who shot and killed at least three of the enemy with his Mauser pistol, was cool and courageous but lucky to survive a bout of hand-to-hand fighting in which 22 British officers and men were killed. Nevertheless he was eager to renew the charge at once. 'Another fifty or sixty casualties would have made our performance historic', he explained to Lady Randolph, 'and made us proud of our race and our blood' (Russell, 225). The charge of the lancers, however, was only a sideshow with no significance for the main battle, which ended in the defeat and mass slaughter of the Dervishes. Up to 11,000 were killed, compared with 28 British officers and men—lancers included.

For a second time Churchill now expanded his war correspondence into a book: *The River War* (1899), a two-volume work in which the story of the campaign was firmly embedded in a remarkably sympathetic history of the Sudanese revolt against Egyptian rule. Churchill wrote:

> Those whose practice it is to regard their own nation as possessing a monopoly of virtue and common sense are wont to ascribe every military enterprise of savage people to fanaticism. They calmly ignore obvious and legitimate motives...upon the whole there exists no better case for rebellion than presented itself to the Soudanese. (Churchill, *River War*, 1973, 22)

Churchill was also critical of aspects of British imperialism. He censured Kitchener for his part in the desecration of the Mahdi's tomb and the slaughter of wounded Dervish soldiers. For all that, he never doubted the 'civilizing mission' of the British in Asia and Africa.

In the spring of 1899 Churchill completed his tour of duty in India, returned home, and resigned his commission. By the time of the outbreak of the South African War, Churchill had negotiated a contract with the *Morning Post* which made him the highest-paid war correspondent of the day, with a salary of £250 per month and all expenses paid. The journalist J. B. Atkins, who sailed to South Africa on the same ship, recalled:

> He was slim, slightly reddish-haired, pale, lively, frequently plunging along the deck 'with neck out-thrust' as Browning fancied Napoleon...when the prospects of a career like that of his father, Lord Randolph, excited him, then such a gleam shone from him that he was almost transfigured. I had not before encountered this sort of ambition, unabashed, frankly egotistical, communicating its excitement, and extorting sympathy. (Atkins, 122)

Hastening to the battle front, Churchill was accompanying an armoured train on a reconnaissance mission in Natal when the train was ambushed (15 November 1899). Revealing once more an ice-cool nerve under fire, he seized command of the situation and organized a successful attempt to free the engine, but was captured and interned with other British prisoners in the States Model School in Pretoria. Later it was sometimes alleged that Churchill gave his word to his captors that if released he would not take up arms against them, and subsequently broke his parole. As no promise to release him was ever made, this was untrue. But he did persuade Captain Aylmer Haldane and Sergeant-Major Brockie to include him in their escape plan, on the understanding that all three would leave together. In the event Churchill climbed out first and, finding that his fellow escapees were unable to join him, set off on his own. After a series of adventures worthy of John Buchan's hero Richard Hannay he escaped via Portuguese East Africa and arrived in triumph in Durban.

Standing out in sharp relief from the military disasters of 'black week', Churchill's exploits made him the hero of the hour. His new fame enabled him to override the objections of the War Office and assume once more the dual role of officer—lieutenant in the South African light horse—and war correspondent. In April 1900 he joined the column commanded by his friend Sir Ian Hamilton as it advanced through the Orange Free State to the Transvaal. Galloping over the veldt with his cousin and boon companion Charles Richard John Spencer (Sunny) Churchill, the ninth duke of Marlborough (1871–1934), fortified by regular supplies from Fortnum and Mason, and attended by his valet, Thomas

Walden, Churchill was often in the thick of the fighting and again proved himself to be a first-class war correspondent. He turned his dispatches, this time with little adaptation, into two books: *London to Ladysmith via Pretoria* (1900), which included the story of his escape, and *Ian Hamilton's March* (1900). The South African War also left an enduring imprint on Churchill's thinking. It convinced him that war was too dangerous to be left to the generals.

# Member of Parliament

# 2

## Hughligan and Free Fooder

While on leave from India during the summer of 1897 Churchill had made contact with Conservative Party managers and delivered his first speech, at Claverton Manor outside Bath (26 June 1897). Two years later, when the sudden death of the MP for Oldham created a vacancy in one of the constituency's two seats, he was adopted as the Conservative candidate at the ensuing by-election, but was defeated by his Liberal opponent. In autumn 1900, when Lord Salisbury decided to call a general election, Churchill again stood for Oldham. This time his fame tipped the balance and he was returned with a small majority. As there was no autumn session of parliament he put the time to good use with a lecture tour of the United Kingdom, followed by a similar tour in the United States and Canada. The story of his escape from the Boers, accompanied by a magic-lantern show, netted him the handsome sum of £10,000, which he handed over to the banker Sir Ernest Cassel to invest on his behalf.

Churchill delivered his maiden speech to the House of Commons on 18 February 1901. While strongly supporting the war in South Africa he caused some alarm on the Conservative benches when he declared: 'If I were a Boer I hope I should be fighting in the field' (Gilbert, *Life*, 139). Having acquired a considerable respect for the Boers he wished to see them offered generous peace terms, a theme he was to emphasize repeatedly over the next few years. Nor was this the only issue on which he diverged from the government. He launched a devastating attack on the secretary of state for war, St John Brodrick, whose proposals for army reform he condemned as increasing military expenditure for no strategic purpose. Imitating the parliamentary tactics once employed by his father, he organized with his friend Lord Hugh Cecil a group of young tory MPs who specialized in the harassment of their own leaders and called themselves the Hughligans. Increasingly in sympathy with the opposition, Churchill was closely in touch with Lords Rosebery and Morley, and other leading Liberals.

Churchill was already a perennial subject of gossip and speculation. Physically he was unimpressive. At 5 feet 6½ inches, slenderly built, with a 31 inch chest, rounded shoulders, delicate skin, ginger hair, and a pugnacious baby face with twinkling blue eyes, he was striking but not handsome. Though he was a fluent writer, he spoke with a lisp and his speeches were the result of long and elaborate preparation. His practice at first was to deliver the whole of a speech from memory, but after an alarming experience in April 1904 in which he 'dried up' in the House of Commons, he never spoke without copious notes. On those who met him he generally made an instant and powerful impression, though not always a favourable one. Hyperactive and transparently on the make, he was far from the English ideal of a gentleman. To many of his fellow officers he appeared pushy and bumptious. Offspring though he was of the landed aristocracy, he belonged to a plutocratic milieu in which old and new wealth rubbed shoulders. His friends included great financiers like Cassel and Baron de Forest, who invited him aboard their yachts for Mediterranean cruises, or played host in magnificent villas and castles on the continent. Churchill enjoyed fox-hunting and country-house weekends but he was equally at home at the gambling tables of the French Riviera. Meeting him for the first time in July 1903, Beatrice Webb thought him 'egotistical, bumptious, shallow-minded and reactionary, but with a certain personal magnetism, great pluck and some originality, not of intellect but of character. More of the American speculator than the English aristocrat' (*Diary*, 287).

When Arthur Balfour succeeded his uncle, Lord Salisbury, as prime minister in May 1902, there was no place in the new government for Churchill. Then in May 1903 Joseph Chamberlain raised the banner of tariff reform. Churchill announced that he was strongly in favour of free trade and soon became one of the most active of the 'free fooders', a group of about sixty Conservative MPs fighting a losing battle for the cause. At the head of a divided party Balfour himself could only procrastinate, a predicament which laid him open to the taunts of Churchill, whose platform speeches combined lucid expositions of political economy with political slapstick. Most Conservative adherents of free trade decided to remain in the party, but Churchill, after some hesitation, crossed the floor of the house and took his seat, next to David Lloyd George, on the Liberal benches (31 May 1904). He had already accepted an invitation from the Liberal Association of North-West Manchester to contest the forthcoming general election as the free-trade candidate. During the next eighteen months, as the Balfour government drifted helplessly towards the rocks, Churchill attacked his former party with a ferocity that gave rise to lasting enmities and the accusation that he was a turncoat.

Churchill shrugged off charges of opportunism. It was the Conservatives, he argued, who had abandoned their principles. For good measure he claimed that he was following in the footsteps of his father, whose life he was then writing. In *Lord Randolph Churchill* (1906), he presented his father as a tory with increasingly radical sympathies, who would probably have opposed the South African War had he lived. His own Liberalism, therefore, could be construed as a continuation of tory democracy. Reviewers were not wholly persuaded by Churchill's portrait of his father as an earnest Victorian statesman, but they acclaimed the book as a literary *tour de force* and a well-documented political history in which the reputations of the living were handled with delicacy and tact.

## New Liberalism and marriage

When Sir Henry Campbell-Bannerman became prime minister in December 1905 Churchill achieved ministerial office for the first time as under-secretary at the Colonial Office. One of his first acts was to appoint the civil servant and scholar Edward Marsh as his private secretary, a role in which he was to serve Churchill in every one of the offices he held between 1905 and 1929. In the ensuing general election the Liberals won a landslide victory and Churchill was elected MP for North-West Manchester.

Since the colonial secretary, Lord Elgin, was a member of the House of Lords, Churchill had the responsibility of handling colonial affairs in the Commons. In March 1906 his first important ministerial speech went badly wrong. While seeking to defend Viscount Milner from a motion of censure over the question of 'Chinese slavery' in South Africa he unwittingly gave the impression of gloating over Milner's downfall, thus rubbing salt into Conservative wounds. Remembered against him for years to come, the episode was an early example of a flaw in his oratorical style: an overbearing manner that seemed intended to humiliate his opponents, of whose injured feelings he was largely unaware. In July he recovered with a statesmanlike speech announcing the restoration of self-government in the Transvaal, a policy to which he had made a significant contribution.

Delighted by his new responsibilities, Churchill ranged inquisitively over the affairs of scores of British colonies, annotating documents with a red fountain pen. As one historian has written: 'He had a generous and sensitive, if highly paternalistic, sympathy for subject peoples, and a determination to see that justice was done to humble individuals throughout the empire' (Hyam, 503). In autumn 1907 he set out on a tour of east Africa which began as a hunting expedition but turned into a semi-official inquiry into colonial affairs. In Kenya he went big-game hunting and investigated the conditions of African contract workers. In Uganda he visited Christian missions, took tea with Daudi Chewa, the eleven-year-old kabaka of Buganda, and took up with great enthusiasm the project for a dam across the Ripon Falls. It would, he concluded:

> be hard to find a country where the conditions were more favourable than in Uganda to a practical experiment in State Socialism . . . A class of rulers is provided by an outside power as remote from, and in all that constitutes fitness to direct, as superior to the Baganda as Mr Wells's Martians would have been to us. (Churchill, *African Journey*, 70–71)

In the interludes Churchill dictated memoranda for the Colonial Office, and a series of articles for the *Pall Mall Gazette*, later published as *My African Journey* (1908). Even in Africa he gave much thought to the future of politics at home and the prospects for the 'new Liberalism' of social reform, which had begun to attract him. On his return home he published an article, 'The untrodden field in politics', advocating a more active role for the state in the economy and the establishment of a national minimum standard to mitigate poverty.

When Herbert Asquith succeeded as prime minister in March 1908 he took the bold step of bringing Churchill into the cabinet as president of the Board of Trade (16 April 1908). At thirty-three, he was the youngest cabinet minister since 1866. Since constitutional convention required that a minister entering the cabinet must resign his seat, Churchill was compelled to contest Manchester North-West for a second time in a by-election, which he lost. He at once accepted an invitation to stand for the safe Liberal seat of Dundee, where he was returned at a by-election in May 1908 and remained MP until 1922.

A great admirer of beautiful women, but self-centred and gauche in their company, Churchill had already proposed to Pamela Plowden and Ethel Barrymore, only to be rejected by both. Then, at a dinner party early in 1908, he was re-introduced to Clementine Ogilvy Hozier (1885–1977), whom he had met briefly once before. Bowled over, he began an ardent courtship. In August he proposed, and was accepted, as they took shelter from the rain in the Temple of Diana overlooking the lake at Blenheim Palace. With Hugh Cecil as best man, and the bishop of St Asaph conducting the ceremony, Winston and Clementine were married at St Margaret's, Westminster, on 12 September 1908.

Churchill expected his wife to be a loyal follower, and it was a role she was content to play. The unhappy child of a disastrous marriage and a financially precarious home, Clementine found in Winston a faithful husband who loved her, sustained her in material comfort, and placed her in the front row of a great historical drama. He could never be accused of marrying for money or running after other women. She, for her part, was never uncritical of her husband or afraid to express her opinions. A lifelong Liberal, with a puritan streak, she never approved of his more louche tory companions such as F. E. Smith, a close friend from 1907 onwards, or Max Aitken, later Lord Beaverbrook, introduced to Churchill by 'F. E.' in 1911. Winston, nevertheless, discussed all his political affairs with her and she often gave him sound advice, which he seldom took. Given the dissimilarities between them, it was not surprising that Winston and Clementine sometimes quarrelled furiously. She once threw a dish of spinach at him, and missed. Nevertheless they were quick to make up after a row, and their marriage was sustained by a lifelong mutual affection expressed in their pet names for each other. Winston was always 'Pug' or 'Pig', Clementine 'Kat', and the children 'the Kittens'. Their first child, Diana, was born in 1909. Their only son, Randolph, followed in 1911, and Sarah in 1914. Marigold was born in 1918, but died in 1921, and the youngest daughter, Mary, was born in 1922.

By the time of his marriage Churchill was working in close alliance with the 'Welsh wizard' David Lloyd George, the chancellor of the exchequer. As Asquith's daughter Violet observed, Lloyd George was undoubtedly the dominant partner:

> His was the only personal leadership I have ever known Winston to accept unquestioningly in the whole of his career. He was fascinated by a mind more swift and agile than his own ... From Lloyd George he was to learn the language of Radicalism. It was Lloyd George's native tongue, but it was not his own, and despite his efforts he spoke it 'with a difference'. (Bonham-Carter, *Churchill*, 161)

Lloyd George encouraged Churchill to concentrate on social policy. Drawing on the advice of his officials he promoted three major reforms: the Trade Boards Act of 1909 which introduced statutory minimum wages into the 'sweated trades'; state-run labour exchanges, planned by the young William Beveridge, whom Churchill recruited as a civil servant specifically for the purpose; and compulsory unemployment insurance, which later became a part of Lloyd George's National Insurance Act of 1911. Though none of these measures was especially controversial in itself, they were part of a wider radical strategy which Lloyd George and Churchill urged on the cabinet, and for which they campaigned at great public meetings. In order to pay for welfare reforms they demanded reductions in the defence budget, precipitating a cabinet crisis over the naval estimates of 1909. Proclaiming something very like their own foreign policy of peace with Germany, they denounced the prophets of a great European war as alarmists. The greatest threat to Britain's imperial might, Churchill declared, was from the internal decay of its people. But Liberalism, in his view, was the antithesis of socialism. 'Socialism seeks to pull down wealth', he declared in May 1908. 'Liberalism seeks to raise up poverty... Socialism would kill enterprise; Liberalism would rescue enterprise from the trammels of privilege and preference' (Addison, *Churchill on the Home Front*, 66).

When in April 1909 the House of Lords took the unprecedented step of rejecting the proposals of the 'people's budget' for increased taxes on the wealthy, Churchill as president of the budget league toured the country denouncing the peers and the Conservative Party. Collected and published in 1909 as *The People's Rights*, his speeches display him at his most radical. Conservatives, of course, detested both Lloyd George and Churchill, but Churchill was the more despised for 'betraying' both his party and his class. Indeed he was ostracized and traduced, as he recalled in old age:

> They said that I beat Clemmie and that you could hear her crying as you passed our house. They said that I drugged, and if you rolled up my sleeve, my arm was a mass of piqures. We were cut by people we had known well and had looked on as friends. (Montague Brown, 147)

The Liberals meanwhile, though grateful for the loan of Churchill's talents, could never forget that he was an aristocrat who had begun his career as a soldier and a tory.

## Home secretary

After the general election of January 1910 Asquith promoted Churchill to the Home Office, where his many responsibilities ranged from the supervision of the Metropolitan Police to the regulation of prisons, borstals, factories, coalmines, and shops. Churchill was eager to pursue an agenda of social reform. Persuaded by the arguments of eugenicists, who maintained that the 'quality of the race' was degenerating due to the multiplication of the 'unfit', he was briefly an enthusiastic supporter of the compulsory sterilization of the 'feeble-minded'. Nothing came of this, but he did secure the passage of a bill to regulate the hours and conditions of shop assistants. In penal policy he made very active use of the home secretary's right to intervene, frequently mitigating the harsh sentences awarded by magistrates for petty crime. A firm believer in capital punishment, he nevertheless agonized over the fate of prisoners under sentence of death and reprieved many of them. His ambitious plans for reducing the number of petty criminals sent to prison were, however, thwarted by the brevity of his tenure of the Home Office.

Churchill's more constructive endeavours as home secretary were overshadowed by controversial problems of law and order. Although he was on record as favouring votes for women in principle, he detested the suffragettes for interrupting his meetings. Warning that he would not be 'henpecked' on the issue, he found reasons to object to the suffrage bill of 1910 and subjected it to a slashing attack in the House of Commons. In November 1910 a suffragette rally at Westminster was met by the police with extremely rough tactics in which several women were injured. Churchill was not personally responsible for 'black Friday', but he rejected all allegations against the police and refused to institute an inquiry.

Within a few days of black Friday a dispute in the south Wales coalfield led to a strike by miners employed by the Cambrian Colliery. Riots and looting broke out in the town of Tonypandy in the Rhondda Valley and one of the rioters was fatally injured in a struggle with the Glamorganshire police. The local magistrates pleaded with the Home Office to authorize the dispatch of troops. Recognizing that any direct clash between troops and strikers might result in bloodshed, Churchill at first refused the request of the local authorities, and sent instead a contingent of the Metropolitan Police. But twenty-four hours later, when it was clear that the riots were continuing unabated, Churchill authorized the dispatch of troops. In a bold and imaginative stroke, which may have been unconstitutional, he appointed General Nevil Macready to command both troops and police, with instructions to ensure that the police acted as a buffer between the strikers and the troops. He thereby took control out of the hands of the local authorities, who might well have been tempted to employ both police and troops as strike-breakers.

Churchill's conduct of the Tonypandy affair prevented further bloodshed, but he was strongly attacked by the Labour Party leader Keir Hardie for condoning brutality on the part of the Metropolitan Police. Afterwards the legend grew that Churchill had sent troops to shoot down striking Welsh miners. Although this was a gross distortion, Churchill's response to industrial unrest was not always cool and measured. During the summer of 1911, when strikes in the docks spread to the railways, he was seized by a nightmare vision of a starving community held to ransom by industrial anarchists. Overriding the local authorities, he dispatched troops to many parts of the country and gave army commanders discretion to employ them. When rioters tried to prevent the movement of a train at Llanelli, troops opened fire and two of the rioters were shot dead. Together with Tonypandy, these events marked a turning point in Churchill's relations with the Labour Party and the trade unions. His record as a social reformer was eclipsed by his new reputation as a class warrior with a 'Prussian' love of order, maintained if necessary by military force.

The impression was deepened by a famous episode in January 1911. Hunted down by the police, a number of Russian anarchists, led by 'Peter the Painter', took refuge in a house in Sidney Street, in the East End of London, and fired at the police. Churchill hastened to the scene, where his conspicuous presence in the danger zone—recorded by a press photographer—led critics to accuse him of seizing operational control from the police. The charge was mistaken. When the house suddenly caught fire, Churchill confirmed the decision of the police to let it burn down, but otherwise he was simply an enthralled spectator whose antics caused much amusement. In the House of Commons Balfour enquired: 'I understand what the photographer was doing, but what was the right honourable gentleman doing?'

(Churchill and Gilbert, 2.409). Though he was still at the forefront of domestic politics, the soldier in Churchill was never far below the surface. As he explained to Clementine in May 1909:

> I would greatly like to have some practice in the handling of large forces. I have much confidence in my judgment on things, when I see clearly, but on nothing do I seem to *feel* the truth more than in tactical combinations. (Soames, 23)

From 1910 onwards, contact with the intelligence services made Churchill apprehensive about German intentions and he began to think seriously about the implications of a major war. At about the same time, and possibly as a consequence, there were signs that he was moving to the right. In September 1910 Lloyd George told Churchill that he had two alternatives for the future: a coalition in which the Liberals and Conservatives reached a compromise over the issues that divided them, and a Liberal government with an advanced land and social policy. Churchill was all for a coalition and henceforth made various efforts to find common ground with his Conservative opponents. With a view to assuaging the bitterness caused by the House of Lords crisis, Churchill and F. E. Smith in May 1911 co-founded the Other Club, a bipartisan dining club of which the Liberal and Conservative chief whips were both members.

# 3

# 'A water creature': the Admiralty

## Navy reforms and the Ulster crisis

The strategist in Churchill was aroused in July–August 1911 by the Agadir crisis when a German gunboat was sent to the Moroccan port. In response Churchill composed for the cabinet an important paper entitled 'Military aspects of the continental problem'. At Asquith's invitation he attended a critical meeting of the committee of imperial defence, which revealed a complete lack of co-ordination between the plans of the Admiralty and the War Office. Much impressed by Churchill's interventions, and by his obvious desire to take charge of the Royal Navy, Asquith moved him from the Home Office and appointed him first lord of the Admiralty in October 1911.

Tradition has it that when an admiral spoke reverently to him of naval tradition, Churchill retorted: 'What are the traditions of the Navy? Rum, sodomy, and the lash!' In later years he explained that he had never said this, but wished that he had. His mission at the Admiralty was to modernize. Many of the reforms he proposed were inspired by the retired first sea lord 'Jackie' Fisher, with whom he was in almost daily contact. But Churchill, of course, also had great confidence in his own judgement and was ready to act boldly.

Churchill's first move was to replace three of the four sea lords. Sir Arthur Wilson was succeeded as first sea lord by Sir Francis Bridgeman, and Prince Louis of Battenberg, a German prince and naturalized British subject, was appointed second sea lord. A dashing young officer, David Beatty, became Churchill's naval secretary. Subsequently, in December 1912, Churchill coerced Bridgeman into retirement, appointing Battenberg in his place. Churchill displayed little respect for many of the senior officers of the Royal Navy, whom he regarded as unimaginative and set in their ways. One of his first actions, in line with Fisher's advice, was to establish a naval war staff of three divisions—operations, intelligence, and mobilization—to prepare and co-ordinate war plans. With the assistance of Herbert Richmond he sought to encourage the interest of naval officers in history and strategy, and helped to launch a new periodical, the *Naval Review*. Eager to explore almost every aspect of naval affairs, Churchill set out to discover the facts for himself. Making frequent use of the Admiralty yacht *Enchantress*—where he also entertained his political friends from time to time—he inspected ships, dockyards, and naval installations with a vigilant eye. In defiance of protocol he sometimes bypassed senior naval officers and sought information directly from junior officers or ordinary seamen.

Many of the admirals were unimpressed. According to the second sea lord, Sir John Jellicoe, Churchill's fatal error was 'his entire inability to realize his own limitations as a civilian ... quite ignorant of naval affairs' (Marder, *From the Dreadnought*, 255). But the admirals, like so many of the experts Churchill was to encounter, were often blinkered by convention. 'In matters of technical advance', writes one historian of Churchill and the navy, 'the First Lord was always in the van, always supporting the pioneers, always sweeping aside the obstruction of the unimaginative' (Gretton, 117). With Fisher's encouragement he developed a fast division of battleships, the Queen Elizabeth class, equipped with the new 15 inch gun. He pressed on with converting the fleet from coal-fired to oil-fired engines. In June 1914 he announced that he had negotiated the purchase by the British government of 51 per cent of the shares in the Anglo-Iranian oil company, thus ensuring a guaranteed supply of oil for the fleet. He promoted the development of submarines and air power, wresting full control of the Royal Naval Air Service from the War Office. In 1913, much to Clementine's alarm, he took up flying lessons and took to the air 150 times, after which she persuaded him to give up flying—for the moment.

Churchill was determined that Britain should retain a clear margin of naval supremacy over Germany. In a speech in Glasgow on 8 February 1912 he argued that for Britain a large navy was a necessity whereas for Germany it was a 'luxury'—a comment which provoked much German anger. When the draft of a new German naval law proposed a further increase in the size of the German fleet, Churchill obtained the cabinet's approval in principle for an expansion of the British naval programme. At the same time he refurbished his Liberal credentials by floating the idea of a 'naval holiday', or joint suspension of naval construction by both countries. Following the German rejection of this idea, Churchill sought a naval arrangement with France under which the British Mediterranean Fleet would be withdrawn and concentrated in home waters, leaving the French to patrol the Mediterranean. Since this would involve the British in a pledge to defend the channel and Atlantic coasts of France, it was tantamount to a military alliance. After long and complex arguments the cabinet agreed in July 1912, but Churchill's expansionist naval policy, and the strengthening of the Anglo-French entente, alienated the radical wing of the Liberal Party and confirmed growing speculation that he was 'moving to the right' or preparing to rejoin the Conservative Party. During the winter of 1913–14 Churchill's insistence on the construction of another four dreadnoughts, and a further increase in the naval estimates, led to a crisis in which he found himself at loggerheads with Lloyd George, the majority of the cabinet, and most of the Liberal Party. Only the delaying tactics of Asquith, and a last-minute decision by Lloyd George to concede most of Churchill's demands, averted his resignation.

As first lord, Churchill tended to concentrate on naval matters to the exclusion of everything else. 'You have become a water creature', Lloyd George told him in July 1912. 'You think we all live in the sea, and all your thoughts are devoted to sea life, fishes and other aquatic creatures' (Riddell, *More Pages*, 78). Nevertheless Churchill was also actively involved in the greatest political issue of the day: Irish home rule. Lord Randolph Churchill had famously declared: 'Ulster will fight, and Ulster will be right'. His son took the opposite line, denouncing Bonar Law and the Conservatives for inciting rebellion. In February 1912 he attempted to confront a Unionist audience in Belfast in the very same hall in which his father had spoken in 1886, but so great was the threat to his safety that the meeting had to be moved at the last minute to the Celtic Road football stadium. In private, however, Churchill made persistent efforts to find a compromise. One possibility, which he proposed in the secrecy of the cabinet room in March 1911, was to include Ireland in an all-round scheme of federal devolution, with seven regional parliaments in England alongside parliaments for Scotland, Ireland, and Wales. The cabinet, however, decided in favour of a single parliament for the whole of Ireland. In September 1912 he caused something of a sensation by airing the concept of federal devolution in a speech in Dundee. By analogy with the seven kingdoms of Anglo-Saxon England, it became known as Churchill's plan to revive the 'heptarchy'. Twice in that same year Churchill urged the cabinet, without success, to offer temporary exclusion from home rule to the predominantly protestant counties. During the winter of 1913–14 he was the principal go-between in a number of secret moves to promote a bipartisan settlement. On the Conservative side his main contact was F. E. Smith, who was both a personal friend and a fervent champion of Ulster. Churchill, it was said, was threatening to quit the cabinet if force were employed against Ulster: 'You understand that if a shot is fired I shall go out' (ibid., 194).

As the hour at which the Home Rule Bill would become law approached, the Ulster Unionists rejected out of hand a belated offer by Asquith to allow the protestant counties to opt out for a six-year period. Churchill now changed tack, arguing that, having obtained a compromise, the Ulster Unionists must accept it. He was also eager to restore his standing in the Liberal Party. In a speech at Bradford on 14 March 1914 he issued a stern warning that Ulster Unionists must agree to the government's plan or take the consequences: 'There are worse things than bloodshed, even on an extended scale', he declared (Rhodes James, 62).

Meanwhile the cabinet was much alarmed by police reports suggesting that the Ulster Volunteers were planning a military coup. A cabinet committee under Churchill authorized precautionary troop movements and Churchill himself, as first lord of the Admiralty, ordered the 5th battle squadron to steam to Lamlash, menacingly close to Belfast. His actions convinced the Conservatives that the government was planning an 'Ulster pogrom'—an impression rapidly confirmed by the notorious episode of the 'Curragh mutiny', when fifty-seven of the seventy officers of the 3rd cavalry brigade declared that they would rather be dismissed than take part in the coercion of Ulster. Churchill often employed provocative language on the public platform while pursuing relatively conciliatory policies behind the scenes. Contemporaries, however, tended to equate extremism of style with extremism of intent. Churchill was partly to blame for the Conservative belief that he had attempted a pogrom.

## Into battle

On the eve of war in July 1914 Churchill wrote to his wife: 'Everything tends towards catastrophe and collapse. I am interested, geared up and happy. Is it not horrible to be built like that?' (Churchill and Gilbert, 2.710). When Austria declared war on Serbia two days later, Churchill, acting with Asquith's approval, ordered the fleets to their battle stations. In the critical cabinet discussions over the next few days

Churchill, the foreign secretary Edward Grey, and the lord chancellor Richard Haldane were consistently in favour of British intervention while others, including Lloyd George, wavered.

According to one historian:

> Churchill took a more active part in the day-to-day running of the war than any First Lord in history. His were many of the ideas for action; it was he who drafted many of the signals to the ships. He studied and analysed each operation with great care. (Gretton, 147)

Churchill's interventionism, which he scarcely bothered to conceal, was a double-edged sword. Though he stood to gain the credit from successful actions by the Royal Navy, he was sure to get the blame when things went wrong. During the first few months of the war the Germans achieved a number of naval successes for which Churchill was strongly criticized. In August two German battleships, the *Goeben* and the *Breslau*, escaped from the Adriatic through the Dardanelles to Constantinople. On 21 September Churchill boasted that if the German fleet did not come out and fight they would be 'dug out like rats in a hole' (Gilbert, *Life*, 281), but on the following day the Germans sank three British cruisers, with the loss of 1459 officers and men, off the Dogger Bank. Two more British cruisers were sunk at the battle of Coronel, off the coast of Chile, on 1 November. On 16 December German battlecruisers shelled Scarborough and other east coast ports, killing or injuring 500 civilians. Criticism of the Admiralty mounted and was only partially offset by successful actions off the Falkland Islands (8 December) and the Dogger Bank (25 January 1915).

Enthralled by all aspects of the fighting, Churchill was eager to play a part in the land war and ingenious in stretching the Admiralty's responsibilities. He converted the naval reserve into the Royal Naval division, an infantry force of 15,000 men, in which many of his friends were commissioned as officers. Although Churchill promised that the division would later be transferred to the control of the War Office, he now had at his disposal something very like a private army. He also established what soon became known as his 'Dunkirk circus', three squadrons of aircraft which bombed German defences from airfields in northern France, protected by a force of Rolls-Royce cars with armour-plating. His response to the deadlock on the western front was to sponsor the idea of a 'land ship', an armoured troop carrier mounted on caterpillars, that would shield them from the field of fire as they approached the enemy trenches. A prototype was housed in the Admiralty basement.

For three-and-a-half days in October 1914 Churchill found himself in virtual command of a land battle. The Germans, advancing rapidly along the channel coast, were threatening the Belgian city of Antwerp. The cabinet dispatched Churchill to organize reinforcements and stiffen the resistance of the Belgian government. Churchill did a superb job organizing the defences of Antwerp and delaying the German advance. No sooner was he on the spot than his fascination with the conduct of military operations gained the upper hand. He called in as reinforcements the bulk of three battalions of the Royal Naval division and fired off a telegram offering to resign his cabinet post in return for a high-ranking command in the field. When Asquith read out the telegram to his colleagues there was a roar of laughter and Churchill was ordered home. The laughter illustrated the gulf between Churchill and the other politicians. The politicians were ultimately responsible for the conduct of the war, but since very few of them knew anything of military matters they relied heavily on the judgement of the generals and the admirals. Inside Churchill, however, was a generalissimo struggling to get out. As Churchill's critics saw it, his military ambitions were foolish and his melodramatic defence of Antwerp a tragic sequel to the farce of Sidney Street. When the city fell he was strongly attacked in the press for the apparent failure of the expedition. This, perhaps, was the moment at which long-held suspicions in the political world hardened into the conviction that he lacked judgement.

## The Gallipoli disaster

In October 1914 the first sea lord, Prince Louis of Battenberg, was forced by anti-German prejudice to resign, and Churchill decided to recall the 73-year-old Fisher to take his place. 'Those who knew them both', wrote E. T. Williams, 'realized that the arrangement involving such domineering characters, each used to having his own way, fond as they were of each other, would not work' (*Dictionary of National Biography*, first edn. 1981). For a time both Churchill and Fisher were excited by the possibility of a naval operation to capture the island of Borkum in the Baltic. But when the Russian government appealed urgently for action to relieve Turkish pressure in the Caucasus, Kitchener, the secretary for war, urged Churchill to undertake a naval demonstration at the Dardanelles. Churchill replied that a naval attack alone would be insufficient: a combined operation would probably be more effective. Kitchener, however, declared that he could not spare any troops, and again pressed the first lord to mount a naval demonstration. Churchill now dispatched a telegram to Admiral Carden, the commander of the Mediterranean squadron, seeking his opinion on whether it would be possible to force the Dardanelles with the aid of obsolete battleships surplus to requirements in home waters. Carden replied that he thought the Dardanelles might be forced by extended operations with a large number of ships. Churchill became captivated by the vision of a fleet sailing through the Dardanelles, bombarding and destroying the Turkish forts and gun batteries on both sides of the straits, and provoking by their appearance in front of Constantinople a revolution and the withdrawal of Turkey from the war. The supply lines to and from Russia through the straits would be opened up, and the Balkan states rallied to the cause of the allies: at a stroke the military balance would be transformed.

Such was the vision. The outcome was a disaster. Both Kitchener and Churchill wavered between the concept of an operation carried out by ships alone, with troops landing subsequently as an occupation force, and a combined naval and military operation. A naval attack was finally launched on 18 March 1915 under the command of Admiral De Robeck. Whether it could ever have succeeded against the dual threat of minefield defences and gunfire from the Turkish forts remains a subject for debate. After the loss of three battleships De Robeck halted the attack and in spite of Churchill's pleas and injunctions refused to renew it. The war council now came down definitely in favour of a combined operation and the purely Churchillian phase of the action was over. After many delays and hesitations, a combined British, Australian, and New Zealand expeditionary force under the command of Churchill's friend Sir Ian Hamilton landed on the tip of the Gallipoli peninsula on 25 April. Within a few days it was clear that the troops were pinned down on a narrow stretch of beach with the Turks shelling them from the commanding heights above. The war council authorized further reinforcements, but there was no disguising the fact that the news was bad.

Fortune now deserted Churchill. From the start, Fisher had blown hot and cold about the Dardanelles. Increasingly overwrought and unstable, and fearful of losses, he suddenly cracked when Churchill, without consulting him, added two submarines from home waters to a list of reinforcements for the Mediterranean. On 15 May Fisher resigned and fled into hiding. Churchill might have weathered the storm but for the fact that Asquith, beset by a crisis over munitions, chose this moment to invite the Conservatives into a coalition. Eager to pay off old scores against Churchill, and fearful of his exploits as an amateur strategist, they insisted on his removal from the Admiralty and the war council. Asquith appointed him chancellor of the duchy of Lancaster, a post that was largely honorific, together with a place on the new Dardanelles committee.

The Gallipoli affair dragged on through the summer and autumn. Though casualties mounted and there was little sign of progress, Churchill continued to champion the operation with unquenchable enthusiasm. By October the majority of the Dardanelles committee had come to the conclusion that the operation should be abandoned and when at last the cabinet decided in favour of withdrawal, Churchill was left with no alternative but to resign from the government. One of the few redeeming features of the Gallipoli affair was the brilliant evacuation with which it was brought to a close in January 1916. By that time, however, some 46,000 allied troops, including 8700 Australians and 2700 New Zealanders, had been killed.

Churchill was, to a great extent, the scapegoat. It was Kitchener who first pressed for a naval operation and Asquith, as prime minister, who authorized it. Fisher concealed his early doubts and subsequently expressed great enthusiasm. Nor did Churchill's responsibility extend much beyond the naval attack on 18 March. The land campaign which began on 25 April was primarily the responsibility of the War Office. Nevertheless Churchill's own egotism and impetuosity were factors in his downfall. He was over-confident of success, trumpeting victory in advance and passionately supporting the operation long after most people had written it off. Gallipoli was a cross to which he nailed himself.

Churchill was devastated by his fall from grace in May 1915. 'Like a sea-beast fished up from the depths', he wrote, 'or a diver too suddenly hoisted, my veins threatened to burst from the fall in pressure' (Churchill, *Thoughts and Adventures*, 307). Nothing could wholly fill the void, but his family proved a great source of strength. Clemmie was a loyal supporter in time of trouble as was Churchill's brother Jack, currently serving at Gallipoli, and his sister-in-law Gwendeline (Goonie). When the Churchills had to leave Admiralty House, they went to live with Goonie and her two children, John and Peregrine, at 41 Cromwell Road. At

> gallery. We could dimly see the table, but walls and roof were invisible. 'Look at it', he said. 'This little place is what makes the difference between us and Germany. It is in virtue of this that we shall muddle through to success & for lack of this Germany's brilliant efficiency leads her to final disaster. This little room is the shrine of the world's liberties. (MacCallum Scott diary, 5 March 1917, Glasgow University Library, MacCallum Scott MSS)

Fearful, perhaps, that Churchill would emerge as the new leader of the opposition, Lloyd George promised to restore him to office. In July 1917, with great difficulty, he obtained Bonar Law's consent to the appointment of Churchill as minister of munitions. Since his new post was outside the war cabinet, this appeared to meet Bonar Law's demand for the exclusion of Churchill from any part in the conduct of the war. Nevertheless 100 Conservative MPs signed a motion deploring his appointment, and the Conservative press complained loudly.

Accompanied by his bust of Napoleon, Churchill moved into the ministry's quarters in the former premises of the Metropole Hotel in Northumberland Avenue. Created by Lloyd George in 1915, it was already in full swing with a staff of 12,000 officials, two and a half million workers employed in its factories, and the output of guns and shells running at record levels. Churchill's brief was to ensure a continuous and increasing flow of production. He began by reorganizing the ministry itself, compressing fifty separate divisions into ten, and creating a munitions council which met daily to co-ordinate and determine policy. The next priority was industrial unrest. Production was threatened by strikes and

Churchill took action to redress some of the most prominent grievances. He abolished the 'leaving certificate' which prevented workers in the munitions trades from moving from one employer to another. More controversially he authorized a 12 per cent bonus for skilled workers on time rates, unwittingly setting off a train of inflationary wage demands as unskilled workers struggled to catch up. Churchill, however, was ready to employ the stick as well as the carrot. In the summer of 1918 he put an end to a strike of engineers in Coventry by threatening to conscript them into the army.

Although Churchill was excluded from the war cabinet, he displayed all the dynamism of a war leader. Determined to investigate for himself the needs of the armies on the western front, he made frequent visits to France for consultations with his French opposite number, Louis Loucheur, and the British commander-in-chief, Sir Douglas Haig. In spite of Churchill's past criticisms of strategy on the western front, he managed to convince Haig that he was doing everything in his power to assist him. He also struck up a firm friendship with Haig's aide-de-camp, Major Desmond Morton, in later years his most important contact in the world of secret intelligence.

Churchill continued to urge that the British and French allied armies remain on the defensive until 1919, by which date the build-up of American forces, together with an overwhelming superiority in tanks, aircraft, gas, and machine-guns, would ensure an allied victory. Lloyd George rejected this advice. But during the crisis of March 1918, when the German offensive in the west threatened to break through the allied lines, he turned to Churchill, dispatching him on an urgent mission to Paris to co-ordinate action with the French premier, Georges Clemenceau. Churchill's own links with France dated back to the days when Mrs Everest had wheeled him up and down the 'Shams Elizzie'. At school he had acquired a fluent but ungrammatical command of French with the vowels pronounced in an emphatically English accent. But his love affair with France seems to have begun in 1907 when he first set eyes on the French army at its annual manoeuvres:

> When I saw the great masses of the French infantry storming the position, while the bands played the 'Marseillaise', I felt that by those valiant bayonets the rights of man had been gained and that by them the rights and liberties of Europe would be faithfully guarded. (Kersaudy, 26)

Both Clemenceau and his great rival, Marshal Foch, made an abiding impression on Churchill. They represented for him, he explained, the dual nature of France: Clemenceau its anticlerical, revolutionary, and republican past, Foch its more ancient, aristocratic heritage of Joan of Arc and the château of Versailles.

## 'Red Peril' and Ireland

The First World War came to an end sooner than Churchill expected. With the Liberal Party split Lloyd George went to the country at the head of a coalition of Conservatives and Coalition Liberals, a group in which he and Churchill were the most prominent figures. In the general election of December 1918 the coalition obtained a stupendous majority and Churchill was again victorious in Dundee.

Churchill hoped to return to the Admiralty, but Lloyd George insisted that he accept the twin posts of secretary for war and air. He was immediately faced with a crisis over demobilization. There was much resentment in the ranks against existing arrangements because they took no account of how long a man had served. So great was the anger that a mutiny broke out at Calais and there were riots at home. Acting with great speed and decision, Churchill introduced a new scheme, based on the principle of 'first in, first out', which defused the discontent.

In the aftermath of war Churchill was haunted by the spectre of the Bolshevik revolution. Soviet communism, he concluded, was the worst tyranny in history and Lenin and Trotsky more dangerous enemies than the Kaiser's Germany. His loathing of communism found expression in the nightmare imagery with which he depicted 'the foul baboonery of Bolshevism' as 'a plague bacillus', a 'cancer', and a 'horrible form of mental and moral disease' (Rose, 146). His greatest fear was that Bolshevism would conquer both Russia and Germany, thus creating a hostile and aggressive bloc stretching from Europe to the Pacific. He therefore urged the victors to adopt a policy of magnanimity and friendship towards Germany: 'Kill the Bolshie, Kiss the Hun', as he put it to Asquith's daughter Violet (Gilbert, *Life*, 412).

Churchill claimed to be carrying out the war cabinet's policy of withdrawing from Russia the 14,000 British troops remaining there at the end of the war. But at a meeting of the supreme allied war council in Paris in February 1919, he argued passionately in favour of a concerted allied attempt to send extra troops, money, and supplies to the white Russian forces. Although he managed to persuade the war cabinet—which remained in being until September 1919—to furnish extra supplies to the white Russians, his repeated pleas in favour of more direct intervention fell on deaf ears. Lloyd George, who was bombarded by Churchill with memoranda on the subject, complained that he was obsessed with Russia to the exclusion of all other issues, but Churchill was unmoved. He was strongly opposed to opening trade negotiations with Russia and hovered on the brink of resignation when an Anglo-Soviet trade treaty was approved by the cabinet in November 1920. Churchill's perceptions of the evils and barbarism of the Bolshevik regime have been vindicated by the passage of time. But after the bloodbath of the First World War neither Britain nor its allies could mobilize the money, the manpower, or the popular consent essential for continued military intervention.

Churchill was also anxious about developments at home. The intelligence services supplied him with intercepts of messages from Moscow authorizing Soviet agents in Britain to subsidize with Russian gold the *Daily Herald*, the British Communist Party, and other left-wing organizations. The *Herald* had already identified Churchill as the labour movement's most dangerous enemy; Churchill, for his part, denounced the Labour Party as unfit to govern, and a prey to the manipulations of extremists.

Preoccupied by the 'red peril', Churchill did not realize until the beginning of 1920 that Ireland was sliding into chaos. The chief of the Imperial General Staff, Sir Henry Wilson, pressed for the introduction of martial law. Churchill, like the rest of the cabinet, was against this, but he gave strong support to Lloyd George's policy of recruiting two paramilitary forces, the Black and Tans and the auxiliary police force, the 'Auxis', who carried out unofficial reprisals against the IRA and also murdered some innocent civilians. When Lloyd George appointed him chairman of a cabinet committee on Ireland in June 1920, Churchill was full of rash ideas for intensifying the conflict including raising a force of 30,000 Ulstermen to maintain British authority throughout Ireland. But as he also explained to the cabinet, his aim was to achieve a position of strength from which constitutional concessions could be granted.

In May 1921 Churchill, by now colonial secretary, urged the cabinet to enter into negotiations on the grounds that British forces now had the upper hand. Two months later Lloyd George called a truce and Churchill was drawn once more into the prime minister's confidence. During the negotiations which led to the Anglo-Irish treaty of 6 December 1921, Churchill was a member of the British delegation and determined to drive a hard bargain. He was chiefly responsible for the military clauses of the treaty, which reserved for Britain three naval bases: the 'treaty ports' as they were later called. His opposite number in the military negotiations was Michael Collins, the leader of the IRA, with whom he established a good working relationship. With the granting of dominion status to the Irish Free State, Churchill as colonial secretary became responsible for Anglo-Irish relations during an extremely tense period in which there was violence along the border between north and south, and the south itself was descending into civil war. Collins feared that in signing the treaty he was signing his own death warrant, and so it proved. But shortly before his assassination in August he sent Churchill a message to thank him for all the support he had given to the precarious government of the Irish Free State during the first few troubled months of its existence: 'Tell Winston that we could never have done anything without him' (Churchill, *World Crisis*, 5.348). Churchill felt a sense of paternity towards the Irish Free State and was greatly affronted when Eamon De Valera came to power in 1932 and began to abrogate the constitutional terms of the treaty. He was even more incensed when Neville Chamberlain returned the treaty ports to Ireland in 1938.

## Palestine, Iraq, and Turkey

Churchill's reputation as a militarist was often at variance with his record in cutting defence expenditure. In the aftermath of the First World War the pressures to reduce public spending were overwhelming. In August 1919 the cabinet adopted, without dissent from Churchill, the 'ten-year rule', whereby military expenditure was to be based on the assumption that there would be no major war for the next ten years. Churchill himself chafed at the expense involved in the British occupation of the former Ottoman territories of Palestine and Mesopotamia (Iraq)—regions which, he told the House of Commons in July 1921, were 'unduly stocked with peppery, pugnacious, proud politicians and theologians …' (Churchill and Gilbert, 4.619). He recommended that the League of Nations mandate for Palestine be given to the United States: it was Lloyd George who insisted that it should go to Britain.

Churchill's drive for a settlement of the Middle East led him to propose that both Palestine and Iraq should be run by a new Middle East department of the Colonial Office. In February 1921, Lloyd George had taken the logical step of appointing Churchill colonial secretary (until April 1921 he also retained the air portfolio), and the new Middle East department was established, with a staff which included T. E. Lawrence. In March Churchill visited Cairo to preside over a conference to settle the affairs of Palestine and Mesopotamia. Although the details of the settlement owed much to others, it was Churchill who took the final decisions. Mesopotamia was transformed into the kingdom of Iraq and the emir Feisal of the Hashemite dynasty was installed as the first monarch. To the dismay of Zionists, Churchill also decided that the whole of Palestine east of the River Jordan should become a second Arab kingdom of Transjordan under Feisal's brother, the emir Abdullah. In accordance with the Balfour declaration of 1917, the League of Nations mandate for Palestine included the provision that Palestine should become a 'national home' for the Jews. Under Churchill's settlement, the promise of a Jewish national home was to apply only to Palestine west of the Jordan, and even then it was to be cautiously interpreted. Though Churchill had been personally sympathetic to Zionism ever since his contacts with Manchester Jews in the Edwardian period, he recognized the need to assuage Arab fears of unlimited Jewish immigration. In a white paper of June 1922, drafted by the British high commissioner in Palestine, Sir Herbert Samuel, but fully endorsed by Churchill, the government declared that the 'Jewish National Home' did not mean 'the imposition of a Jewish nationality upon the inhabitants of Palestine as a whole' but the continued development of the existing Jewish community (Rose, 157).





Churchill could point to great achievements, but they failed to dispel doubts and reservations about him. The general consensus was well expressed by a political commentator who wrote in 1920:

> Unhappily for himself, and perhaps for the nation, since he has many of the qualities of real greatness, Mr Churchill lacks the unifying spirit of *character* which alone can master the discrepant or even antagonistic elements in a single mind, giving them not merely force, which is something, but direction, which is much more. He is a man of truly brilliant gifts, but you cannot depend upon him. His love for danger runs away with his discretion; his passion for adventure makes him forget the importance of the goal. (Begbie, 103)

The Lloyd George coalition was essentially an alliance between Lloyd George himself and the Conservative Party, a temporary arrangement which left the Coalition Liberals insecure. Both Lloyd George and Churchill sought a way out of the problem by advocating 'fusion'—an amalgamation of the two wings of the coalition to form a new centre party based on resistance to socialism. Churchill campaigned strongly for this during the first half of 1920, at a time when the Conservatives might have accepted the idea, but it foundered on the opposition of many Coalition Liberals. After this, Lloyd George and Churchill could only hope to find some means of prolonging the life of the coalition.

50 In 1920, with the enthusiastic support of Lloyd George, but much against the will of Churchill, the allies had imposed on the Turks the draconian treaty of Sèvres. In response Turkish nationalists under the leadership of Mustapha Kemal rose up against the treaty and began to force the Greeks into retreat. Up to this point Churchill had taken a robustly pro-Turkish line. But in August 1922 Turkish forces drove the Greeks into the sea and advanced towards the British garrison at Chanak on the eastern shore of the Dardanelles. For about a fortnight it looked as though the garrison might be attacked or overrun, and the cabinet decided on 29 September to instruct Sir Charles Harington, the British commander on the spot, to deliver an ultimatum to the Turks. Churchill, by this time, was an excitable member of the war party in the cabinet: he did not mean to suffer a second humiliation at the Dardanelles. When Harington decided not to deliver the ultimatum the Chanak crisis petered out, but the government's warlike stance was highly unpopular and helped to seal the fate of Lloyd George's tottering regime. At the Carlton Club meeting on 19 October, Conservative MPs voted to bring down the coalition and fight the general election as an independent party.

# Swashbuckling Conservative

# 5

## 'Without an office, without a seat'

Churchill, who had been operated on for appendicitis, was too ill to take part in the opening stages of the election. Clementine bravely stood in for him but quickly discovered that the mood of the electorate had turned ugly. When a pale and fragile Churchill at last arrived he had to be carried to the platform on a makeshift sedan, and address the audience seated. He was howled down. He and his fellow Liberal candidate were defeated by the Labour candidate, E. D. Morel, and the veteran prohibitionist Edwin Scrymgeour. 'In the twinkling of an eye', Churchill was to write, 'I found myself without an office, without a seat, without a party, and without an appendix' (Churchill, *Thoughts and Adventures*, 213).

Churchill had also been going through a troubled phase in his family life. In April 1921 Clementine's brother, William Hozier, shot himself in a hotel in Paris. The following June, Lady Randolph died suddenly after the amputation of a leg. The most shattering blow for Winston and Clementine was the death from septicaemia in August of their youngest daughter, Marigold ('the Duckadilly'), aged two years nine months. At the end of 1921 Clementine collapsed from nervous exhaustion. 'What changes in a year!', Churchill wrote to her, 'What gaps! What a sense of fleeting shadows! But your sweet love and comradeship is a light that burns. The stronger as our brief years pass' (Soames, 203). Before long there was cause for rejoicing after all. On 15 September 1922 Clementine gave birth to their fifth and last child, Mary.

After the fall of the coalition Churchill withdrew to the south of France. Ever since 1918 hecklers had been interrupting him at public meetings with the cry of 'What about Gallipoli?' Determined to confound the critics, he set to work with astonishing speed and energy on a mammoth history of the First World War. The first volume of *The World Crisis*, published in April 1923, was devoted mainly to his reorganization of the Royal Navy between 1911 and 1914. In the second, which appeared six months later, he concentrated on Gallipoli and the argument that it was a strategically sound concept flawed by errors and tricks of fate for which he was not responsible. The main theme of the third part, published in two volumes in March 1927, was his measured critique of Haig's strategy on the western front. A fifth volume on the crises of the immediate post-war period, *The Aftermath*, appeared in March 1929, and a sixth, *The Eastern Front*, in November 1931.

Although parts of *The World Crisis* were highly autobiographical, drawing on documents from Churchill's private papers, the book as a whole was a stupendous narrative of the war in Europe featuring masterly set-piece accounts of major battles. Dictated to secretaries as he strode up and down the room, it exhibited his passionate interest in war and his romantic conception of the 'true glory' of the troops who perished on the Somme. But he could not write of the blood-baths on the western front without sombre reflections on the growing destructive power of modern warfare: 'Mankind has never been in this position before. Without having improved appreciably in virtue or enjoying wiser guidance, it has got into its hands for the first time the tools by which it can unfailingly accomplish its own extermination' (Churchill, *World Crisis*, 5.454).

The writing of *The World Crisis* proceeded in parallel with the restoration of Churchill's political fortunes. In May 1923 his old opponent Bonar Law was succeeded as prime minister and leader of the Conservative Party by the more accommodating Stanley Baldwin. Churchill's hopes of reunion with the Conservatives were temporarily blocked when Baldwin declared in favour of protection and called a general election in December 1923. Standing for the last time as a Liberal, at Leicester West, Churchill was defeated by the Labour candidate. When the Liberals decided to support a minority Labour government under the leadership of Ramsay MacDonald, Churchill seized the chance of putting himself at the head of the many right-wing Liberals who would have preferred an anti-socialist alliance. He issued a statement declaring: 'The enthronement in office of a Socialist Government will be a serious national misfortune such as usually has befallen great states only on the morrow of defeat in war' (Pelling, 287). In the Westminster Abbey by-election of March 1924 Churchill entered the fray as an 'independent anti-socialist', and almost beat the Conservative candidate. Having served notice that he was still a force to be reckoned with, he was shortly afterwards adopted by the local Conservative association as the 'constitutionalist' candidate for the safe Conservative seat of Epping.

In the ensuing general election of October 1924 the Conservatives were returned with a substantial overall majority, Churchill's own majority at Epping being nearly 10,000; he held the seat until his retirement in 1964. To Churchill's astonishment Baldwin—whose aim was to detach him from Lloyd George—asked him whether he would accept the Treasury. Churchill recalled,

> I should have liked to have answered, 'Will the bloody duck swim?', but as it was a formal and important conversation I replied, 'This fulfils my ambition. I still have my father's robe as Chancellor. I shall be proud to serve you in this splendid office.' (Churchill and Gilbert, 5.59)

## The Exchequer: gold standard and general strike

Having taken office on 7 November 1924, Churchill's first major decision as chancellor of the exchequer delighted the Bank of England, the Treasury, and the Conservative Party. In the budget of April 1925 he announced the restoration of the gold standard at the pre-war parity of $4.86 to the pound. Warned against this step by Lord Beaverbrook and John Maynard Keynes, Churchill conducted a thorough investigation into the arguments for and against before coming to the conclusion that the decision was inevitable and possibly right. The consequence, however, was an overvalued pound, which had damaging effects on British export industries, including coal, and thus precipitated the general strike. So, at least, historians have tended to argue and Churchill himself, in later years, came to regard the restoration of the gold standard as a disastrous mistake.

In financial policy Churchill was in principle a Gladstonian Liberal committed to free trade, strict economy in public expenditure, and balanced budgets. On free trade he demonstrated some flexibility, accepting the relatively minor instalments of protectionism that had already been introduced, but rejecting the demands of tariff reformers like L. S. Amery for protective duties on iron and steel. He launched a vigorous drive for reductions in public spending, outraged the Admiralty by compelling reductions in its cruiser programme, and refused to finance the construction of a naval base at Singapore. For what, he asked in a letter to Baldwin (15 December 1924), was the Admiralty preparing? 'A war with Japan! But why should there be a war with Japan? I do not believe there is the slightest chance of it in our lifetime' (Churchill and Gilbert, *Companion*, vol. 5, pt 1, p. 306). In June 1928 the cabinet accepted Churchill's proposal that the ten-year rule should be placed on a permanent basis, advancing day by day until such time as a decision was taken to revise it.

Churchill set his face firmly against the radical programme of public works advocated by Lloyd George and the Liberals as the solution to unemployment. Nevertheless he brought to the annual budget a showmanship reminiscent of the Welsh wizard. In his first budget he was able to announce a substantial cut in income tax, coupled with a new scheme (devised by the minister of health, Neville Chamberlain) of widows' and orphans' pensions. In 1927 he was captivated by the idea of derating—abolishing local authority rates on industry—which he hoped would act as a powerful stimulus to trade and industry. But his proposals led to prolonged battles with Chamberlain. The final scheme, announced by Churchill in the budget of 1928, was a compromise. Industry and the railways were to be freed of 75 per cent of local authority rates, and agriculture of 100 per cent, but a new tax of 4*d*. in the pound on petrol was introduced as partial compensation for the loss of revenue. Derating proved to be a damp squib and was subsequently abandoned by the second Labour government.

Wherever he turned, Churchill found that his hopes for economic expansion were thwarted. Like previous chancellors, he tried hard to cut through the tangle of war debts and reparations which had arisen out of the First World War, but found the United States unwilling to cancel the debts incurred by Britain and France. He also complained about the strict monetary policies of the Bank of England under its governor, Montagu Norman. Even more alarming was the prospect of the harm that might be done to the economy through industrial strife. In June 1925 Churchill averted a major strike in the coal industry by agreeing to a nine-month Treasury subsidy for miners' wages. But this was a temporary measure to give both sides in the coal industry a breathing space in which to reach a settlement. When the nine months expired without a settlement there was no question of any more state subsidies. And when the general council of the Trades Union Congress called a general strike

(May 1926) in support of the miners, Churchill was determined to break the strike.



So too were Baldwin and the rest of the cabinet. If Churchill appeared more militant than his colleagues it was because he was more rhetorical and demonstrative. Baldwin put him in charge of an emergency government newspaper, the *British Gazette*, to which he contributed unsigned editorials that breathed defiance. When he arranged for troops to convoy supplies from the London docks through the streets, rumour had it that he was itching to put down the strike by military force. After nine days the strike petered out, but the dispute in the coal industry lingered on, with very little attempt by Baldwin to resolve it. Churchill had always distinguished clearly between the general strike, which he regarded as a challenge to the constitution, and the coal dispute, which he regarded as purely industrial. In the autumn, while Baldwin was away on holiday, Churchill intervened and tried to put pressure on the coal owners to settle, but was thwarted by powerful interests in the Conservative Party.

To the alarm of the Foreign Office, Churchill continued to keep a close watch on the international scene. He remained bitterly hostile to the Soviet Union and rejoiced when diplomatic relations were broken off after the Arcos raid. More surprising, given his long-standing commitment to the improvement of relations between Britain and the United States, he passed through a brief phase of anti-Americanism, prompted by naval rivalries. Nor was Churchill a Francophile at this period. When the foreign secretary, Austen Chamberlain, proposed an Anglo-French alliance, Churchill came out strongly against the idea. According to Sir Eyre

 Crowe, he was all for letting France 'stew in her own juice' (Blake and Louis, 53).

In September 1922 Churchill paid £5000 for a new home. Chartwell Manor, near Westerham in Kent, was a dilapidated house, built on a hilltop overlooking the Weald of Kent, with 80 acres of land including a valley and a lake. Captivated by the view, Churchill acted without the agreement of Clementine, who disliked the house but nevertheless worked hard to make the best of it. After hiring the architect Philip Tilden, Churchill began to pour a fortune into the renovation, redesign, and extension of Chartwell. By the spring of 1924 it was ready for occupation.

Chartwell was Churchill's first permanent home. Here he could enjoy family life and the company of his friends in a more spacious and hospitable setting, but the house was also his political headquarters. Among those who soon became frequent visitors were F. A. Lindemann ('the Prof'), professor of experimental philosophy (physics) at Oxford, and Brendan Bracken, a youthful Irish adventurer mistakenly rumoured to be Churchill's illegitimate son. Both were attracted by his swashbuckling Conservatism and love of adventure. In Churchill himself, Chartwell brought out a hitherto unsuspected love of the land. He experimented with the raising of pigs, chickens, and other livestock, investing large sums with very little return. He took up bricklaying and was recruited by a local branch official as a member of the Amalgamated Union of Building Trade Workers, but the union's executive, failing to share the joke, ruled that he was ineligible for membership.

## India die-hard





In the general election of May 1929 the Baldwin government lost its overall majority and was succeeded by a second minority Labour government, dependent for office on the support of the Liberals. Churchill sought vainly for a Liberal-Conservative alliance against the government. In August 1929 he sailed with his brother Jack and his son Randolph to Canada, which he traversed from east to west as a guest of the Canadian Pacific Railway. After a visit to the Calgary oilfields, Randolph criticized the oil magnates for their lack of culture. Churchill rebuked him: 'Cultured people are merely the glittering scum which floats upon the deep river of production!' (Churchill, *Twenty-one Years*, 74).

As the Conservatives edged towards protectionism, Churchill's free-trade credentials were a waning asset and he was much in need of a new rallying cry to restore him to the front line of the political battle. He found it in the defence of British rule in India. In October 1929 the viceroy, Lord Irwin, declared that the ultimate goal of British rule in India was 'dominion status'. To Churchill's dismay Baldwin endorsed the Irwin declaration, and supported a round-table conference of British and Indian representatives to discuss constitutional reform. Although Churchill was prepared to accept a measure of self-government at the provincial level, he was passionately opposed to the idea of an all-India federation with an element of self-government at the centre. After months of tension the final break between Churchill and Baldwin came in January 1931, when Gandhi and other Congress politicians were released from gaol to enable them to attend the round-table conference.

Resigning in protest from the shadow cabinet, Churchill launched into a campaign to mobilize the tory backbenches and the constituency activists against Baldwin.

Whether or not Churchill's aim was to seize the leadership of the Conservative Party, there is no reason to doubt the strength of his convictions on the subject. Churchill believed that British rule in India was a guarantee of good government and the protection of the masses. Self-government, he predicted, would lead to exploitation, corruption, and communal strife between Muslim and the Hindu. Unlike the viceroy and his officials, who were in touch with the political realities, he failed to appreciate the strength of the nationalist movement. The Congress leaders, he imagined, could be swept aside in a vigorous display of imperial will: attempts to appease them would only increase their appetite for power. He declared on 23 February 1931:

> It is alarming and also nauseating to see Mr Gandhi, a seditious Middle Temple lawyer, now posing as a fakir of a type well-known in the East, striding half-naked up the steps of the Viceregal Palace while he is still organising and conducting a campaign of civil disobedience, to parley on equal terms with the representative of the King-Emperor. (Gilbert, *Life*, 499)

In October 1930 Churchill published *My Early Life*, a witty and elegiac account of his youth shot through with regret at the decline of the social and imperial order in which he had grown up. Parliamentary politics, Churchill felt, were now in the hands of lesser men drifting on the fickle currents of a mass electorate. What was needed was strong leadership both at home and in India. As Baldwin wrote in November

1930: 'He wants... the Tory party to go back to pre-war and govern with a strong hand. He has become once more the subaltern of Hussars of '96' (Davidson, 355). When Baldwin and MacDonald joined forces in the National Government of August 1931, Churchill's views on India ensured his exclusion from office.

Churchill was visiting the United States on a money-making lecture tour when he was knocked down by a car and badly injured while attempting to cross Fifth Avenue in New York (13 December 1931). Had he been killed he would perhaps be remembered today as the most illustrious and interesting failure in twentieth-century British politics. Instead he recovered and returned home to resume his India campaign. In April 1933 he turned down an invitation to join the joint select committee appointed to examine and report on the government's proposals for constitutional reform. Though he seldom enjoyed the support of more than sixty backbench MPs, it was a different story in the constituencies, where he and his fellow diehards organized, through the India Defence League, a highly effective campaign of subversion. At the annual party conference they won a third of the vote in October 1933 and nearly a half in October 1934. The battle reached a climax in the 1934–5 session of parliament, as the secretary for India, Samuel Hoare, struggled to pilot the Government of India Bill through the Commons. Though it reached the statute book, it had already been wrecked by the refusal of the Indian princes to participate in the federal provisions of the new constitution: hence the all-India federation to which Churchill had objected so strongly was never to materialize.

# 6 The Nazi threat

## Rearmament and collective security

Churchill's India campaign distracted attention from his simultaneous warnings over the rise of Hitler's Germany. Churchill was horrified by the brutally repressive character of the Nazi regime and repelled by its antisemitism, which he frequently condemned in his speeches. 'I remember', Clement Attlee recalled, 'the tears pouring down his cheeks one day before the war in the House of Commons, when he was telling me what was being done to the Jews in Germany' (*Churchill by his Contemporaries*, 23). But it was the external ambitions of the Nazis, not their internal policies, that caused Churchill most alarm. With fascism as such—a loose term which covered a variety of regimes—he had no quarrel. In February 1933 he praised Mussolini, at that time a potential ally of Great Britain, as 'the greatest lawgiver among living men' (Churchill and Gilbert, 5.457). While recognizing Germany's legitimate grievances over the treaty of Versailles, Churchill argued that it would be folly for the victors to disarm before the grievances of the vanquished were redressed. He therefore condemned the attempts made by the British government and the international disarmament conference in Geneva (1932–4) to reduce Britain and France's armed forces to the level of Germany's. If Germany were granted equality in armaments, he warned the House of Commons in April 1933, 'so surely should we see ourselves within a measurable distance of the renewal of general European war' (Rhodes James, 287). Following the withdrawal of Germany from the League of Nations and the disarmament conference in autumn 1934, he strongly opposed unilateral concessions like the Anglo-German naval treaty of 1935. Diplomacy, he argued, must be backed by military force. From 1934 onwards he campaigned for rearmament in the air with the aim of achieving parity of front-line strength between the RAF and the Luftwaffe.

Churchill's campaign was fuelled by information leaked to him, probably in breach of the Official Secrets Act, by high-level civil servants who feared that the pace of rearmament was too slow. One of his principal informants was his old friend Desmond Morton, whose role as director of the Industrial Intelligence Centre was to monitor the economic preparations that Germany and other European countries were making for war. Another was Ralph Wigram, the head of the central department of the Foreign Office, which had its own intelligence sources. Both Morton and Wigram supplied Churchill with secret estimates of German aircraft production which appeared to contradict Baldwin's pledge that parity in the air would be maintained. In the House of Commons, Churchill gathered around him a formidable body of Conservative supporters and pressed the government hard in powerful speeches, full of detailed allegations, that sent shock waves through the cabinet. Although he was out of office, Churchill was no outsider. As a privy councillor and elder statesman he always had access to the inner circle and was often consulted on matters of defence. In September 1934, when Stanley Baldwin was on holiday at Aix-les-Bains, Churchill and F. A. Lindemann called in to see him and urged the establishment of a high-powered committee to inquire into the problems of defence against air attack. Their initiative led to the setting up of the air defence research committee of the committee of imperial defence. When Baldwin succeeded Ramsey MacDonald as prime minister in June 1935 he invited Churchill to serve on the air defence committee, of which he remained a member up to the outbreak of war in 1939. Churchill was therefore well briefed on the development of radar and Fighter Command's plans to combat the Luftwaffe.

On some aspects of defence Churchill's judgement was questionable. The intelligence assessments that both he and the government received greatly overestimated the front-line strength and capabilities of the German air force. 'No more than his informants', wrote D. C. Watt, 'did he realise that the capacities of the aircraft in production in Germany and Britain up to 1939 made it impossible for either country to launch a serious bombing attack against the other from bases in their own territory' (Watt, 204). In spite of the part he had played in the invention of the tank, he was unaware of the revolutionary doctrines of tank warfare adopted by the German army. His faith in the French army was unshakeable but misplaced. After a tour of the Maginot line in August 1939 he wrote:

> The French front cannot be surprised. It cannot be broken at any point except by an effort which would be

> enormously costly in life and would take so much time that the general situation would be transformed while it was in progress. (Gilbert, *Companion*, vol. 5, pt 3, p. 1594)

Consequently Churchill paid little attention to the state of the army or the need to prepare a properly trained and equipped expeditionary force. As for naval warfare, Churchill accepted the Admiralty's over-optimistic assessments of the ability of warships to defend themselves against attack from the air, and the effectiveness of the ASDIC detection device in reducing the menace posed by submarine warfare. Churchill prophesied war, but not the kind of war the British were compelled in the end to fight.

In Churchill's view, all other threats were eclipsed by the danger from Nazi Germany. Acts of aggression by other nations might therefore have to be tolerated or condoned. When Italy attacked Abyssinia in 1935 he was torn between expressions of support for the League of Nations and the desire to maintain friendly relations with Italy as a potential counterweight to Germany. The outbreak of war between China and Japan in 1937 seems to have caused him little anxiety, as he was largely oblivious of the threat posed by Japan to the British empire in the Far East.

By 1936 the India question was out of the way, the government was pressing on with rearmament, and there were large areas of foreign policy—such as the need for non-intervention in the Spanish Civil War—on which Churchill agreed with the cabinet. There was much talk of Churchill's imminent return to office, though Baldwin failed to appoint him, in March 1936, to the newly created post of minister for the co-ordination of defence. But new differences between Churchill and the government were beginning to emerge. In principle at least, the cabinet fully accepted the need to give priority to the air defence of Great Britain. But Churchill argued that measures to defend the homeland, however essential, were no substitute for the establishment of a military balance of power on the continent. Following the German remilitarization of the Rhineland (to which he reacted with studied moderation), Churchill therefore began to call for Britain to take the lead in the pursuit of collective security through the League of Nations, a policy that opened up the possibility of co-operation with the Soviet Union. And although he continued to base himself mainly on the Conservative Party, he began to reach out—with the assistance of a cross-party organization, the Focus—for Liberal and Labour support.

In December 1936 Churchill's campaign for 'arms and the covenant' was interrupted by the abdication crisis. His plea for Edward VIII to be given more time to reach a decision was mistakenly interpreted by conspiracy theorists as an intrigue to overthrow Baldwin, and his reputation suffered. When Baldwin finally departed in May 1937, Churchill welcomed his successor, Neville Chamberlain, and warmly seconded his nomination as leader of the Conservative Party. At first he was slow to realize that Chamberlain's policies were diametrically opposed to his own. Anthony Eden's resignation from the Foreign Office in February 1938 gave him cause for concern and he stressed the need for an Anglo-French alliance, but when the Czech crisis came to a climax in September 1938 he continued up to the last minute to hope that Chamberlain and the new Foreign Secretary, Lord

Halifax, would adopt his own policy of a 'grand alliance' with France and the Soviet Union to deter Hitler. Only after the Munich agreement did Churchill break decisively with Chamberlain. Speaking in the Commons he declared: 'We have suffered a total and unmitigated defeat ... What I find unendurable is the sense of our country falling ... into the orbit and influence of Nazi Germany and of our existence becoming dependent on their good will or pleasure' (Churchill and Gilbert, 5.999–1000).

## In the wilderness

During the winter of 1938–9, the true period of Churchill's exile in the wilderness, he was ostracized by his own party and narrowly survived a vote of confidence in his constituency association. Even Eden, and the small group of MPs who followed him, held aloof. After the German occupation of Prague in March 1939, however, Churchill's stock began to recover rapidly. By the summer a number of newspapers, including the *Daily Telegraph*, were campaigning for his recall to office. Churchill now applauded Chamberlain's apparent change of policy while strongly urging a Soviet alliance, a course the prime minister was loath to follow.

Driven as much by financial need as by political motives, Churchill devoted much of the 1930s to literary endeavours. In 1929 he began work on the life of his ancestor the first duke of Marlborough. Churchill had the advantage of exclusive access to the Blenheim archives, and the services of the young Maurice Ashley as his research assistant. But the book owed its force to Churchill's deep knowledge of high politics and military operations, his mastery of the source materials, and his passionate desire to vindicate his ancestor's character from the charges levelled against him by Lord Macaulay. Published in four volumes between October 1933 and September 1938, *Marlborough: his Life and Times* took its place at once among the classics of historical writing. As the story of his ancestor's leadership of a grand alliance to prevent the domination of the continent by a single power, it was also a source of inspiration to Churchill in his campaign against appeasement. He also signed a contract in 1932 for another multi-volume work, *A History of the English-Speaking Peoples*, for which the publishers Cassell agreed to pay an advance of £20,000. Setting himself a target of 1000 words a day, he began work on the book on 1 August 1938. By the outbreak of war in September 1939, when plans for publication had to be suspended, there were 530,000 words in proof and the book was almost finished. In the intervals between writing history and making it, he poured out a stream of articles for the press, including a series of biographical profiles later collected and published as *Great Contemporaries* (1937). His weekly commentaries in the *Evening Standard*, syndicated throughout Europe by a Hungarian Jew, Emery Reves, were published in book form as *Step by Step* (1939).

Churchill was probably the highest-paid English author of his day, but his earning powers were rarely sufficient to meet the bills resulting from his extravagant spending habits. 'To run his estate efficiently,' wrote one of his biographers, 'Churchill was helped by eight or nine indoor servants, a nannie or governess, two secretaries, a chauffeur, three gardeners, a groom, and a working bailiff' (Rose, 193). In spring 1938 losses on the stock market compelled him to put Chartwell up for sale, but he was rescued by the generosity of the financier Sir Henry Strakosch, who agreed to cover his share losses and take control of his American investments.

Churchill's marriage to Clemmie endured, but there were many storms as the children grew up. The uncontrollable Randolph veered between adoration of his father, drunken escapades, and rash political initiatives, like his intervention in the Wavertree by-election of January 1935. Diana's marriage in 1932 to John Bailey ended in divorce after three years, though she subsequently married the Conservative MP Duncan Sandys, who became a loyal follower of Churchill. Both Winston and Clementine were horrified when Sarah Churchill, who had become a successful actress, defied them by marrying a divorced Viennese entertainer, Vic Oliver: 'He did not impress me with being a bad man,' wrote Churchill after their first encounter, 'but common as dirt' (Soames, 412). Later he became fond of his son-in-law and was distressed when the marriage broke up.

## 'Winston is back'

The outbreak of war in September 1939 compelled Chamberlain to offer Churchill a place in the war cabinet. He was thrilled to return, as first lord of the Admiralty, to the very same post he had occupied in August 1914. 'Winston is back', the Admiralty signalled to the fleet, or so tradition has it—no record of the signal has ever been found.

The overall direction of the war was now in the hands of Chamberlain and the war cabinet, acting on the advice of the new military co-ordination committee chaired by Lord Chatfield. Chamberlain, who was fearful at first of Churchillian intrigues, was surprised to discover that the first lord of the Admiralty was a remarkably loyal colleague. For the first and only occasion, Mr and Mrs Churchill and Mr and Mrs Chamberlain dined together. Nevertheless the two politicians were rivals. While Chamberlain seemed ill at ease as a war minister, Churchill's beaming face and flamboyant style threatened to eclipse him.

Churchill's dynamism quickly made its mark at the Admiralty. He ordered that all naval vessels should be fitted with radar and all merchant ships armed. Confident that the U-boat menace would rapidly be overcome, he announced figures for German losses which his advisers knew to be greatly exaggerated. When Captain Talbot, the director of anti-submarine warfare, queried the figures, Churchill telephoned him to say:

> There are two people who sink U-boats in this war Talbot. You sink them in the Atlantic and I sink them in the House of Commons. The trouble is that you are sinking them at exactly half the rate I am. (quoted in *Sunday Times*, 13 July 1980)

In April 1940 Talbot was dismissed on Churchill's instructions (Roskill, 94).

Churchill sought a daring role for the navy. Apparently unaware of the danger posed by bombers to ships without fighter cover, he repeatedly pressed the naval staff to adopt a hair-raising plan, eventually thwarted by the first sea lord, Admiral Pound, to send a naval force into the Baltic.

Another idea that captured his imagination was the mining of Norwegian coastal waters to prevent the transport of Swedish iron ore to Germany. After the Russian invasion of Finland on 30 November 1939, he urged the dispatch of an expeditionary force to Narvik to seize the Swedish ore fields, under the pretext of going to the aid of Finland. Not until the end of March 1940 did the supreme allied war council authorize the mining of the leads. On 9 April, German forces marched into Denmark and Norway.

Chatfield having resigned a few days before, Churchill at Chamberlain's request now took the chair of the military co-ordination committee and began to dominate operations. An expeditionary force under the command of Admiral Cork was dispatched to Narvik but a few days later Churchill decided to open up a second front around Trondheim, and the rear half of the convoy was diverted to central Norway. When Churchill suggested a naval bombardment of Narvik, the land commander, General Mackesy, protested that it would be shameful to bombard thousands of Norwegian men, women, and children. Churchill signalled to Cork: 'If this Officer appears to be spreading a bad spirit through the higher ranks of the land forces, do not hesitate to relieve him or place him under arrest' (Marder, 'Winston is back', 54). After further rapid changes of plan on Churchill's part the forces sent to the Trondheim area were overwhelmed and evacuated.

# 7

# 'Walking with destiny'

## Prime minister

Churchill's critics began to murmur that the Norway fiasco was a second Gallipoli, but this time the deeper political currents were in his favour. Chamberlain and his colleagues had been in office since 1931. They could no longer escape the blame when disaster struck. On 8 May 1940, the second day of the parliamentary debate on Norway, Churchill wound up with a strong fighting speech in defence of the government. But when the house divided, the government's majority fell from its normal level of more than 200 to 81, a decisive moral defeat.

Chamberlain realized that a coalition government was now inevitable, and that in the likely event of Labour refusing to serve under him he would have to resign. But who was to be the successor? The alternative leader preferred by the 'establishment' was the foreign secretary, Lord Halifax, and there is some evidence to suggest that initially Churchill was prepared to serve under him. At 4.30 p.m. on 9 May, Chamberlain called a meeting to discuss the succession, the others present being Churchill, Halifax, and the Conservative chief whip, David Margesson. Chamberlain and Margesson raised the question and waited for the others to speak. Churchill, however, had been urged by the cabinet member Kingsley Wood, and possibly Brendan Bracken as well, not to disclaim the succession. Churchill therefore said nothing, and after a brief silence Halifax explained the reasons why he did not think a member of the House of Lords should be prime minister. Churchill had won the premiership with scarcely a hint of intrigue or disloyalty.

When Chamberlain awoke next morning to the news that Germany had invaded Belgium, he imagined at first that he could stay on, but his fate was sealed by a message from the Labour Party reiterating its refusal to serve under him. On Chamberlain's advice Churchill was summoned to the palace and at six o'clock that evening he accepted the king's invitation to form a government. 'It was the irony, or fatality of history', wrote Liddell Hart, 'that Churchill should have gained his opportunity of supreme power as the result of a fiasco to which he had been the main contributor' (Taylor and others, 187). In ruling circles his appointment as prime minister was generally regarded as a gamble, and a dangerous one at that, but Churchill himself was confident. 'I felt', he wrote, 'as though I were walking with destiny and that all my past life had been a preparation for this hour and for this trial' (Churchill, *Second World War*, 1.527).

Churchill immediately invited the Labour and Liberal parties to join a coalition government. At the top he set up a war cabinet of only five members consisting of himself and the leaders of the two main parties: Chamberlain and Halifax for the Conservatives, Clement Attlee and Arthur Greenwood for Labour. Although he found room in his administration for non-party figures like Lord Woolton and John Anderson, the government he established was based firmly on the party system, with a balance maintained between Conservative and Labour, and a whips' office staffed jointly by the two parties. The leader of the Liberals, his old friend Archie Sinclair, came in as secretary for air. To begin with, the war cabinet was based on the Lloyd George model of 1916, with four of its five members free of departmental responsibilities. But Churchill gradually moved away from this: by January 1941 there was a war cabinet of eight, of whom four were departmental ministers.

While avoiding a purge, Churchill began to disperse the inner circle of the 'men of Munich'. Sir Horace Wilson, the head of the Treasury and *éminence grise* of the Chamberlain regime, was banished from 10 Downing Street. Samuel Hoare was sent into exile as ambassador to Madrid, and John Simon removed to the Lords as lord chancellor. Chamberlain, however, stayed on as lord president, retaining the leadership of the Conservative Party, and Halifax continued as foreign secretary. Churchill brought in Ernest Bevin, the general secretary of the Transport and General Workers' Union, as minister of labour, to mobilize the trade unions behind the war effort. And in fulfilment of his long campaign for rearmament in the air, he stripped the Air Ministry of its responsibility for the manufacture of aircraft and transferred it to a ministry of aircraft production under his old friend Lord Beaverbrook.

Like most incoming prime ministers, Churchill arrived with his own 'kitchen cabinet' of personal advisers, consisting principally of Bracken, his parliamentary private secretary; F. A. Lindemann, his scientific adviser, who became head of the prime minister's statistical section; and Desmond Morton, his liaison officer with the intelligence services. John Colville, one of Chamberlain's private secretaries, stayed on to become a devoted Churchillian, and the author of a diary which remains the most intimate and authoritative portrait of Churchill as prime minister. At the request of the war cabinet, the Harley Street physician Sir Charles Wilson, later Lord Moran, was appointed in May 1940 to watch over the prime minister's health. When Churchill crossed the Atlantic in December 1941 he took his doctor with him, and subsequently Wilson accompanied the prime minister on all his travels. He supplied Churchill with sleeping pills and other prescriptions, and summoned the appropriate consultants whenever the prime minister fell seriously ill. 'To his unfailing care', Churchill wrote after the war, 'I probably owe my life' (Churchill, *Second World War*, 3.556). The notes Moran took of conversations with his patient, including confidential details of his medical history, later formed the basis of a controversial book, *Winston Churchill: the Struggle for Survival, 1940–1965* (1966).

## 'Finest hour'

In his first speech in the House of Commons as prime minister, on 13 May 1940, Churchill said: 'You ask, what is our aim? I can answer in one word: it is victory, victory at all costs, victory in spite of all terror, victory, however long and hard the road may be' (Churchill and Gilbert, 6.333).

With the French army already in retreat, Churchill authorized the dispatch of additional fighter squadrons to France and flew to Paris to investigate the position for himself. When he asked the French commander-in-chief, General Gamelin, 'Où est la masse de manoeuvre?', he was appalled when Gamelin replied: 'aucune'. With no realistic prospect of a counter-attack, Churchill's priority was to prevent the encirclement of the British expeditionary force (BEF) under Lord Gort. He ordered Gort to retreat towards Dunkirk and the garrison at Calais to fight to the end to delay the German advance.

While the fate of the BEF hung in the balance, the war cabinet discussed an Italian offer to mediate between Germany and the allies, with the implication that Britain and France would enter into negotiations with Germany. Halifax, supported at first by Chamberlain, argued in favour of exploring the Italian proposal. Churchill, while not in principle ruling out the possibility of negotiations, was passionately opposed on the ground that any terms Hitler was likely to offer would be unacceptable. To strengthen his position he summoned a meeting of ministers outside the war cabinet and was loudly applauded when he declared: 'If this long island story of ours is to end at last, let it end only when each one of us lies choking in his own blood upon the ground' (*War Diary*, 28). By the evening of 28 May, Churchill had won the crucial debate in the war cabinet. Within a few days the bulk of the BEF had been successfully evacuated from Dunkirk.

In June 1940 Churchill flew twice to France in a fruitless effort to persuade the French government to fight on. In a last-minute bid to revive their morale he even grasped at the idea of a declaration of perpetual union between Britain and France and proposed this to the Reynaud government, which turned it down. Reynaud was succeeded by Marshal Pétain, who at once concluded an armistice with Germany. When the French fleet in harbour at Oran refused to surrender to the Royal Navy, Churchill ordered it to be bombarded and sunk (4 July 1940). Meanwhile, on 17 June, General Charles de Gaulle had arrived in London proclaiming himself the leader of the 'Free French'. Overriding much opposition from within his own government, Churchill gave him official recognition and built him up as a rallying point for opposition to the Pétain regime.

Fearful that the Nazis would be assisted from within by a 'fifth column', Churchill ordered a mass round-up of enemy aliens. Between May and July about 22,000 Germans and Austrians were interned, a panic measure which he soon began to regret. As German air attacks intensified in July and August 1940 he toured the country, inspecting coastal defences and Fighter Command bases in the eye of the storm. On his instructions the Local Defence Volunteers were renamed the Home Guard, and eventually supplied with arms. But there was little Churchill could do to alter the course of the battle of Britain. His most important contribution at this point was the bracing effect of his presence, and most of all of his speeches, on the morale of government and people.

Churchill's speeches during the summer and autumn of 1940 were the most inspired and inspiring of his long political life. Contrary to folk memory he made few broadcasts at this period, and there is no evidence to support the claim that the BBC employed the actor Norman Shelley to impersonate him. When he promised 'blood, toil, tears and sweat' (13 May) or vowed that 'we shall fight on the beaches' (4 June), he was addressing the House of Commons only, though he went on to make recordings of this and other wartime speeches after 1945. The same was true of his tribute (20 August) to the fighter pilots of the battle of Britain: 'Never in the field of human conflict was so much owed by so many to so few' (Churchill and Gilbert, 6.333, 468, 742). After the fall of France, however, he reluctantly agreed to repeat over the radio a speech made earlier in the day in the house. Families gathered around the wireless therefore did hear him say, on 18 June: 'Let us therefore brace ourselves to our duty and so bear ourselves that if the British Empire and its Commonwealth lasts for a thousand years, men will still say: "This was their finest hour"' (ibid., 571).

Churchill's patriotic rhetoric aroused the emotions, but his speeches also commanded attention for a different reason. They pierced the fog of rumour and speculation with vivid and authoritative commentaries on the military and strategic situation. Although there was a strong propaganda element in his presentation of the facts, and many secrets lay concealed, they were the speeches of a great parliamentary democrat, leading, informing, and instructing a nation. Not everyone was impressed or won over. There were pockets of society where pre-war mistrust of Churchill lingered, and old wounds festered. By July 1940, however, opinion polls recorded that 88 per cent of the public approved of him as prime minister, a phenomenally high level of support that continued throughout the war.

It nevertheless took some time for Churchill to establish his authority in Whitehall and Westminster. During the first few weeks of the new government the applause for Churchill came from the Labour benches while the majority of Conservatives displayed their loyalty to Chamberlain. As Churchill's stature grew during the summer and autumn of 1940 he achieved a personal ascendancy over all parties, but when Chamberlain retired through ill health in September 1940 Churchill prudently arranged for his own election as leader of the Conservatives. He thereby obtained control of the majority party in the house, an essential power-base if he were to weather the storms ahead. The sequel followed in December when the British embassy in Washington fell vacant. Churchill sent Halifax to Washington, replacing him as foreign secretary with Anthony Eden.

## Conducting the war

Churchill's authority was great but he never sought or possessed the powers of a despot. As a general rule he was punctilious in seeking the support of the war cabinet for major decisions in foreign, imperial, or domestic policy, and there were times when his colleagues overrode his wishes. The war cabinet, however, soon lost control over the military conduct of the war. On becoming prime minister Churchill took the title of minister of defence, and the military secretariat of the war cabinet and the chiefs of staff committee were incorporated into an embryonic department under his personal direction. His defence office was headed by Major-General Hastings Ismay and his two deputies, Colonel Leslie Hollis and Colonel Ian Jacob. Working under their direction were the joint planning committee and the joint intelligence committee, whose task it was both to propose operations and to report on the feasibility of plans submitted to them by Churchill and the chiefs of staff. Ismay also served as Churchill's representative on the chiefs of staff committee, which continued to meet separately. But as minister of defence Churchill had the right both to summon the chiefs of staff and to give them instructions on the conduct of the war.

The new machinery for the conduct of the war owed much to Churchill's thinking, and proved highly successful in preventing the rifts between 'frocks' and 'brasshats' which had occurred in the First World War. At first Churchill called frequent meetings of the defence committee of the war cabinet—which consisted of Attlee, Beaverbrook, and the three service ministers—but as his power grew it was summoned less and less, and the three service ministers were relegated to administrative roles. Thereafter Churchill ran the military side of the war himself in conjunction with the chiefs of staff committee, the most significant of all the checks and balances limiting his power. With his buccaneering spirit, colossal energy, and fertile imagination, he drove his professional advisers hard, and sometimes to distraction. His favourite was the first sea lord, Admiral Pound, whose dogged loyalty was, however, tempered by devious methods of resistance. It was much to Churchill's credit that the service chiefs he himself appointed were sturdily independent characters: Sir John Dill in succession to Sir Edmund Ironside in May 1940, Sir Charles Portal in succession to Sir Cyril Newall in October 1940, and Sir Andrew Cunningham in succession to Pound in September 1943. Dill clashed with Churchill once too often and was removed in

December 1941, but in his place Churchill appointed Sir Alan Brooke, of whom he remarked: 'When I thump the table and push my face towards him, what does he do? Thumps the table harder and glares back at me' (Alanbrooke, xvi). Though Churchill often tried to bully Brooke into submission, he never forgot the fatal consequences of Admiral Fisher's resignation in 1915, and seldom overruled the chiefs of staff on a strategic issue.

Within a fortnight of taking over as prime minister, Churchill acquired 'a source of undreamed-of power; knowledge to use against the unsuspecting enemy, but also a trump card in his negotiations with his Chiefs of Staff and allies' (Stafford, 189). On 22 May the code-breakers at Bletchley Park broke the main operational key of the Luftwaffe's Enigma enciphering machine. This marked the beginning of Ultra, the daily flow of transcripts of radio messages sent by the German armed forces. Though Ultra was continuously monitored and reported on by the joint intelligence committee, Churchill insisted that he should have direct and independent access to the raw materials. In September 1940 the head of the Secret Intelligence Service, Sir Stewart Menzies, was instructed to send all the original transcripts in a daily box to the prime minister. As the volume of transcripts grew, Churchill authorized Menzies to send him a selection only, but he continued to receive a box of what he called his 'golden eggs' on almost every day of the war. The wartime expansion of British intelligence services, and the high repute they acquired in Whitehall, owed much to Churchill's support.

# Grand strategy

# 8

## Looking to America

When Italy declared war on Britain on 10 July 1940 a new theatre of operations opened up in the Middle East. The following month, at great risk to home defence, Churchill sent 154 tanks to Egypt to reinforce Sir Archibald Wavell, the British commander-in-chief. He was now in charge of a promising war against a lesser enemy in a distant theatre. But how was Britain to defeat Germany? As yet he could not tell. In the vain hope of opening up a line of communication with Stalin he sent a prominent left-wing politician, Sir Stafford Cripps, as ambassador to Moscow. Inspired by a vision of the occupied peoples of Europe rising up against their Nazi oppressors, he authorized the creation of the Special Operations Executive (SOE) to 'set Europe ablaze' (*War Diary of Hugh Dalton*, 62). To harass the enemy he ordered commando raids around the coasts of occupied Europe. Churchill also believed in the importance of strategic bombing, but his main hopes were pinned on the prospect of American intervention.

In October 1939 President Roosevelt had initiated a correspondence with Churchill and the two had exchanged a handful of messages on naval matters. Once Churchill became prime minister the correspondence, in which he signed himself 'Former Naval Person', assumed an altogether new significance. Churchill had long possessed a romantic faith in the common destiny of the 'English-speaking peoples': the British empire and the United States. Perhaps because of this, there was more than a touch of wishful thinking in his view of Roosevelt. He tended to exaggerate the extent of the president's commitment to Britain. Addressing a secret session of the House of Commons on 20 June he predicted that once the forthcoming presidential election was over, 'the whole English-speaking world will be in line together' (Churchill, *Secret Session Speeches*, 15). Nevertheless Churchill's view of the United States was grounded in military and strategic reality. As he repeatedly reminded Roosevelt, the defeat of Britain, and the capture or destruction of the Royal Navy, would lay the United States open to attack by Nazi Germany. Hence the United States must come to the aid of Britain in order to defend itself.

Churchill's most important achievement in the summer of 1940 was to convince Roosevelt and his advisers that the British had the will to fight on and were therefore worth supporting. Nevertheless he was impatient for more American aid than he received. The 'destroyers for bases' deal was of greater military value to the United States than to Britain. In December 1940 Churchill sent Roosevelt a long, detailed, and urgent request for military supplies. Roosevelt responded by proclaiming the principle of lend-lease, enacted by congress in March 1941, whereby the United States supplied Britain with food, weapons, and other essentials on credit for the duration of the war. Lend-lease was a lifeline for the future, but Churchill's hopes of an early American entry into the war were disappointed.

In May 1940 the prime minister and the president were still virtually strangers. They had met once before, at a banquet in Gray's Inn in 1918, but to Roosevelt's chagrin Churchill had forgotten the occasion. The arrival in London of Harry Hopkins in January 1941 marked the beginning of a closer relationship in which Churchill dealt informally with trusted intermediaries of the president like Hopkins himself and Averell Harriman. When he was entertaining important American visitors, Churchill was the most generous and agreeable of hosts and one of the most persuasive of propagandists—but he too was susceptible to charm offensives. His first wartime meeting with the president, an event carefully stage-managed for the benefit of a global audience, took place aboard a British battleship, the *Prince of Wales*, at Placentia Bay off Newfoundland, on 9 August 1941. Churchill came away momentarily convinced that Roosevelt was about to bring the United States into the war, but within a few days he realized that he had read too much into the president's warm words. One tangible outcome of the meeting was the Atlantic charter, a rather nebulous joint declaration of war aims. But from Churchill's point of view a more important consequence was the extension of American activity in the battle of the Atlantic: for much of 1941 the threat posed by U-boats to Britain's Atlantic lifeline was the greatest of all his anxieties.

When Greece was invaded by Germany in March 1941, Churchill accepted the advice of Eden and Wavell and sent in British and Commonwealth troops, but in April Greece was overrun. In May, Crete in turn was invaded and captured and British forces were again evacuated. Meanwhile German Panzer divisions under the command of Rommel had arrived in north Africa. When a British counter-offensive failed in June 1941 Churchill ran out of patience with Wavell and replaced him as commander-in-chief Middle East with General Claud Auchinleck. During the autumn of 1941 Churchill bombarded the chiefs of staff with projects for landings on the coasts of Norway, Sicily, Italy, and French north Africa. Conversely he paid little attention to the Far East, discounting the idea that Japan would dare to attack the United States or the British empire. Even if they did attack, he believed, the defences of Singapore would be strong enough to withstand assault for at least six months. Churchill was the driving force of British grand strategy, but his butterfly imagination, fluttering from one attractive prospect to another, drove Brooke to the verge of despair. 'He cannot grasp the relationship of various theatres of war to each other', he wrote in May 1943. 'He always gets carried away by the one he is examining and in prosecuting it is prepared to sacrifice most of the others' (Alanbrooke, 401).

## 'Action this day'

It is scarcely an exaggeration to say that between June 1940 and December 1941, Churchill carried the world on his shoulders. The burdens he bore, and the anxieties he endured, would have crushed many a lesser mortal. When Auchinleck was summoned home to explain why he had not yet taken the offensive, Ismay took him aside and briefed him about the prime minister. He explained:

> Churchill could not be judged by ordinary standards; he was different from anyone we had ever met before, or would ever meet again. As a war leader, he was head and shoulders above anyone the British or any other nation could produce. He was indispensable and completely irreplaceable... He was a child of nature. He venerated tradition, but ridiculed convention. When the occasion demanded, he could be the personification of dignity; when the spirit moved him, he could be a *gamin*. His courage, enthusiasm and industry were boundless, and his loyalty was absolute. No commander who engaged the enemy need ever fear that he would not be supported. (Ismay, 269–70)

Conversely, Churchill could be ruthless in his treatment of commanders he deemed lacking in offensive spirit. He warmed to the dash and charm of Harold Alexander, and the maverick qualities of Orde Wingate, but the self-effacing and the inarticulate found little favour. Dill he described as 'the dead hand of inanition' (Alanbrooke, xv). Of Wavell he remarked: 'It may be my own fault, but I always feel as if in the presence of the chairman of a golf club' (Lewin, 57). Of his dealings with the admirals, Captain Roskill wrote: 'Churchill wielded the executioner's axe so indiscriminately, and with so little attempt to ascertain whether his intended victims really were incompetent, that the injustices perpetrated were not few' (Roskill, 278).

When Chamberlain was prime minister, the business of government was conducted through formal meetings at prearranged times. Under Churchill, the formal business was only a small part of the story. As Edward Bridges, the secretary to the war cabinet, recalled:

> There were no frontiers between home and office, between work hours and the rest of the day: work went on everywhere, in his study, in the dining-room, in his bedroom. A summons would come at almost any hour of the day or night to help in some job. Minutes would be dictated, corrected, re-dictated. One might find oneself unexpectedly sitting in the family circle or sharing a meal while one took his orders. (Bridges, 95)

Within the intimacy of the inner circle, he was a man of transparent emotions and changeable moods. Another civil servant who observed him at close quarters describes how, when he took the chair at a meeting,

> that child-like face became the reflection of the man—the set bulldog look, the sulky look of a pouting child, the angry violent look of an animal at bay, the tearful look of a compassionate woman, and the sudden spontaneous smiling look of a boy. (Mallaby, 29–30)

Churchill usually began the morning's work in his bedroom, going through his boxes, telephoning, and summoning people to see him. Visitors would find him sitting up in bed in a dressing gown emblazoned with dragons, top-secret papers strewn over the bedclothes, and a favourite cat curled up at his feet. From time to time he would dictate to a secretary a series of minutes for dispatch to all corners of Whitehall. The more urgent, which caused great alarm to the recipients, carried a label with the instruction 'action this day' printed in red capitals. If there were no meetings of the war cabinet or other appointments Churchill would sometimes work in bed all morning. Over lunch, at which friends and family rubbed shoulders with politicians and military chiefs, Churchill would discourse on the war, or anything else that came to mind, with a bottle of champagne—he had been a loyal customer of Pol Roger since 1908—followed by brandy. After lunch he would retire for a siesta while everyone else continued to work. By the late afternoon he was a giant refreshed, sipping a whisky and soda, and ready for another round of meetings followed by dinner with more champagne and brandy. His early training as a soldier had taught him to abhor drunkenness and there is 'no credible testimony of Churchill's being drunk, in the falling-down slurred-words sense, while he was Prime Minister' (Kimball, *Forged in War*, 22). But Churchill was clearly dependent on alcohol, and capable on occasion of absorbing quantities that would have rendered lesser men incapable—a feat that stood him in good stead at Kremlin banquets.

If Churchill was spending the weekend at Chequers or Ditchley Park the guests were often invited to join him in watching a film. His favourite, produced in Hollywood by his friend Alexander Korda, was *That Hamilton Woman*, with Laurence Olivier as Nelson and Vivien Leigh as Lady Hamilton. By this time it was nearly midnight and Churchill was ready to return to work. Struggling to keep their eyes open, his advisers would be summoned to a meeting at which key strategic or operational issues were discussed and informal decisions reached. Churchill's 'midnight follies', as they were known in Whitehall, caused much resentment among the exhausted officials who were compelled to attend them. Often Churchill would work until three or four in the morning before taking his sleeping capsules and retiring to bed.

When he was not driving his officials to the limit, Churchill was the most visible of prime ministers, with a showmanship that upstaged the shy and stammering George VI. He strode through the blitzed areas with a bulldog expression in which anger and sorrow were mingled. His most famous theatrical prop was a large Havana cigar, which he would light and flourish with much ceremony, but seldom smoke. His most famous gesture, the V-sign with the palm of the hand turned outwards, was an adaptation of a notoriously rude gesture. In addition to his normal Westminster attire of bow-tie and striped suit, he appeared at various times in the uniforms of air commodore, elder brother of Trinity House, and colonel of hussars. Early on in the war he gave up wearing a dinner jacket in favour of a zip-up 'siren' suit which he sometimes wore in public, an eccentricity for which he was criticized by Aneurin Bevan. On official trips he was often accompanied by Clementine, whose Aid to Russia Fund also made her prominent in her own right. With Mary serving in the ATS, Sarah in the WAAF, and Randolph a staff officer in the Middle East, later parachuted into Yugoslavia as a special envoy to Tito, Churchill's own family played a notable supporting role. In October 1939 Randolph had married Pamela Digby. In symbolic defiance of Hitler, their son, Winston Spencer Churchill, was born at the height of the London blitz (10 October 1940). The marriage, however, was short-lived, and the relationship between Randolph and his father continued to be fraught.

'We have a deep animal love for one another', Churchill reflected, 'but every time we meet we have a bloody row' (Churchill and Gilbert, 8.308).

## Prospects of victory

From intelligence sources Churchill was aware in the spring of 1941 that Germany was planning to invade Russia. By the time operation Barbarossa was launched on 22 June his own response had been carefully thought out. That same day he broadcast from Chequers declaring that Britain would send all possible aid to Russia, a promise he made strenuous efforts to fulfil. While concealing the existence of Ultra he authorized the sharing of secret intelligence with Moscow and the dropping by SOE of Soviet agents into Europe. In September he dispatched Beaverbrook to Moscow on a mission to ascertain Soviet needs. At a time when every tank and gun was urgently required in Britain, the chiefs of staff were reluctant to accept the diversion of resources to Russia, but Churchill intervened to ensure that key supplies were sent by convoy through the Arctic.

Churchill's dealings with the Soviet Union touched on a dilemma at the heart of his war leadership. Between the wars he had strongly opposed socialism and communism. But in order to defeat Hitler he was compelled to ally with forces subversive of the world in which he believed. If this were true at home, where the coalition inaugurated a form of 'war socialism' of which Labour and the trade unions were the main beneficiaries, the contradiction between Churchill the anti-Bolshevik and Churchill the Soviet ally was even more stark. In his broadcast of 22 June Churchill refused, as he put it, 'to unsay one word' he had said against communism in the past. But as he had remarked only the day before: 'If Hitler invaded Hell, he would make at least a favourable reference to the Devil!' (Colville, *Fringes of Power*, 404). As Stalin's ally he was compelled to remain silent about the horrors of the Soviet system. When Stalin demanded formal British recognition of the Soviet frontiers of 1941, Churchill narrowly escaped an embarrassing surrender.

Churchill had no advance warning from intelligence services of the Japanese attack on Pearl Harbor on 7 December 1941, the news of which was confirmed for him by the butler, Sawyers, who had heard it on the radio. Churchill was overcome with joy and relief. 'So we had won after all! . . . Hitler's fate was sealed. Mussolini's fate was sealed. As for the Japanese, they would be ground to powder. All the rest was merely the proper application of overwhelming force' (Churchill and Gilbert, 3.539). Within a week Churchill set sail for the United States with a high-powered delegation on board the *Duke of York*. At a series of meetings in Washington, Churchill and Roosevelt established a combined chiefs of staff representing both countries. On 26 December, Churchill received a rapturous reception when he addressed a joint session of both houses of congress. 'I cannot help reflecting', he declared, 'that if my father had been American, and my Mother British, instead of the other way round, I might have got here on my own' (ibid., 7.29). From Washington, Churchill travelled to Ottawa where he put on another bravura performance in a speech to the Canadian parliament. In 1940, he recalled, the French generals had told their prime minister: ' "In three weeks England will have her neck wrung like a chicken". Some chicken!',

Churchill declared to thunderous applause, 'some neck!' (ibid., 7.34).

Although Churchill was now certain of ultimate victory, the immediate prospects were grim. In the hope of deterring Japan from entering the war he had dispatched the *Prince of Wales* and the *Repulse* to the Far East. On 10 December 1941 Japanese torpedo bombers sank them both. In a bitter contrast two German battleships, the *Scharnhorst* and the *Gneisenau*, successfully ran the gauntlet of British air power in the channel. On 15 February 1942 Singapore and its garrison of 130,000 British and Commonwealth troops surrendered, a body blow from which the British empire was never to recover. Until a few weeks previously Churchill had been ignorant of the fact that Singapore had no landward defences. 'I ought to have known', he wrote. 'My advisers ought to have known and I ought to have been told, and I ought to have asked' (Churchill, *Second World War*, 4.43).

Though Churchill won a vote on confidence in the house by a majority of 464 to 1 on 29 January, he was threatened by powerful undercurrents of discontent and the emergence of Sir Stafford Cripps, newly returned from Moscow, as a potential rival. Bowing to the pressure, Churchill reconstructed his government, bringing Cripps into the war cabinet. Shortly afterwards he dispatched Cripps to India on a mission to negotiate a constitutional settlement with Gandhi and the Congress Party. As Churchill may well have calculated in advance, the mission failed and Cripps's reputation was diminished.

When in April 1942 Roosevelt sent George Marshall and Harry Hopkins to London to persuade the British to agree to a cross-channel invasion that same year, or possibly in 1943, Churchill appeared to be enthusiastic and full agreement was reached in principle. The British chiefs of staff, however, believed that an invasion in 1942 would be premature and disastrous. Gradually, Brooke convinced Churchill that the route to victory lay through Italy via north Africa. Visiting Washington in June, Churchill persuaded Roosevelt to agree to an alternative: operation Torch, an Anglo-American landing in north Africa.

Churchill was at the White House when the news arrived of another British disaster: the surrender of Tobruk. Although he defeated a motion of censure in the House of Commons by 475 votes to 25 (2 July 1942), he was well aware that he was on trial, and might not survive another great military defeat. In August he flew out to Egypt with Brooke to reorganize the Middle East command. Auchinleck was replaced by Harold Alexander and Bernard Montgomery put in command of the Eighth Army. From Cairo Churchill flew on to Moscow for his first meeting with Stalin, who was urgently demanding the opening up of a second front in Europe. Explaining to Stalin that there would be no cross-channel invasion in 1942, Churchill drew on all his powers of persuasion to impress on him the significance of Anglo-American plans for the strategic bombing of Germany and the invasion of French north Africa. Drawing a sketch of a crocodile, he explained to Stalin that it was Anglo-American strategy 'to attack the soft belly of the crocodile as we attacked the hard snout' (Churchill and Gilbert, 4.433). To Churchill's relief, Stalin immediately grasped the strategic importance of Torch and the visit to Moscow ended cordially with a Kremlin banquet lasting seven hours.

The monthly opinion polls continued to register a phenomenally high approval rating for Churchill as prime minister of around 80 per cent, and there was scarcely a murmur against him in the national press. Within the political élite, however, there was much discontent accompanied by pressures to restrict his powers as minister of defence in a fashion that he would have found impossible to accept. 'The Prime Minister', Brendan Bracken told Moran, 'must win his battle in the desert or get out' (Moran, 72). Montgomery's decisive victory at El Alamein, followed by the success of the landings in north Africa, transformed both the military prospects and Churchill's own fortunes. He ordered the church bells to be rung for the first time since 1940 (15 November 1942), and pugnaciously declared: 'I have not become the King's First Minister in order to preside over the liquidation of the British Empire' (Churchill and Gilbert, 7.254).

# 9

# National victory, personal defeat

## Strategic bombing and the Holocaust

Churchill was still not certain how the war would be won. Sir Charles Portal, the chief of the air staff, and Sir Arthur Harris, the commander-in-chief of Bomber Command from February 1942, were fervent believers in the theory that Germany could be defeated by strategic bombing alone. They were supported by Churchill's scientific adviser, Professor Lindemann, who submitted a paper in March 1942 arguing that bombing would destroy Germany's power of resistance by making one-third of her population homeless. Churchill never wholly accepted this theory. Generally speaking he strongly supported the strategic bombing offensive, and the vast production programme it entailed, but he saw it as an essential precondition for the invasion of the continent, not as an alternative. 'Even if all the towns of Germany were rendered largely uninhabitable', he wrote to Portal in October 1941, 'it does not follow that the military control would be weakened or even that war industry could not be carried on' (Gilbert, *War Papers*, 3.1313).

96 The British government never admitted that it was deliberately bombing civilians, but reports of the scale of the destruction visited on German towns and industrial areas made the truth fairly obvious. A handful of dissenters condemned the policy on ethical grounds, and Churchill himself suffered occasional pangs of conscience. In June 1943 he was watching a film of bombing raids on German towns when he suddenly exclaimed: 'Are we beasts? Are we taking this too far?' (Churchill and Gilbert, 7.437). After the destruction of Dresden in February 1945 led to public controversy, Churchill wrote a memorandum in which he argued that 'the moment has come when the question of bombing of German cities, simply for the sake of increasing the terror, though under other pretexts, should be reviewed' (ibid., 7.1257). Dismayed by this apparent attempt to dissociate himself from a policy for which he had been largely responsible, Portal persuaded Churchill to withdraw and revise the minute.

By autumn 1941 Churchill was aware from intelligence reports of Nazi atrocities against the Jews on the eastern front. He spoke out against Nazi war crimes and called for the prosecution of the guilty after the war. In a public letter to the archbishop of Canterbury (29 October 1942) he declared:

> The systematic cruelties to which the Jewish people—men, women and children—have been exposed under the Nazi regime are amongst the most terrible events of history. Free men and women denounce these vile crimes, and when this world struggle ends with the enthronement of human rights, racial persecution will be ended. (Churchill and Gilbert, 7.245)

Nor were these the only signs of Churchill's pro-Jewish sympathies. During the first eighteen months of the war he was strongly in favour of arming the Jews, a policy which eventually led to the creation of a Jewish brigade in 1944. He persuaded the war cabinet to accept in principle the partition of Palestine, and the creation of a separate Jewish state, thus overturning the policy of the Chamberlain government. In spite of all this, some historians argue that Churchill's government could and should have done more to assist the Jews. Some accounts acquit him of responsibility on the ground that his wishes were thwarted by powerful forces in Whitehall; others assert that he could have overcome the opposition if he had summoned up the political will to do so. Either way there is no disputing the fact that his sympathy for the Zionist cause wavered for a time after the assassination by Jewish terrorists in November 1944 of his close friend Lord Moyne, the minister of state in the Middle East.

In August 1941 Churchill authorized a top-secret programme of research, code-named Tube Alloys, into the production of a British atom bomb. Meanwhile parallel research was in progress in the United States. In June 1942 Churchill and Roosevelt reached an unwritten agreement to make nuclear research a joint enterprise with free exchange of information and the sharing of results. Disputes then arose when the Americans cut off the supply of information but these were resolved by Churchill and Roosevelt in the Quebec agreement of 19 August 1943. The free exchange of scientific data was resumed and it was agreed that no information should be given to any other power. With his usual concentration on the military issues at the expense of post-war questions, Churchill formally disclaimed all British interest in the industrial and commercial applications of the project. It was also agreed that neither Britain nor the United States would use the bomb without obtaining the other's approval. Churchill's consent to the use of nuclear weapons against Japan was sought and received (4 July 1945) before the bombing of Hiroshima and Nagasaki. In all this he acted without informing or consulting the war cabinet.

## Churchill's allies

Churchill and Roosevelt met on nine different occasions and spent about 120 days in each other's company. During the second half of 1942 and the first half of 1943 Churchill persuaded the American president to pursue a Mediterranean strategy in preference to the alternative of an early cross-channel invasion favoured by the American chiefs of staff. But when Churchill and Roosevelt met at Quebec in August 1943, Churchill's desire to reinforce the Italian campaign caused sharp differences, fuelling American suspicions that he wished to avoid a cross-channel invasion altogether. At the Tehran conference (27 November to 2 December 1943), Roosevelt joined Stalin in rejecting Churchill's Mediterranean schemes, which included the seizure of Rhodes, the opening up of supply lines to Tito and the partisans, and (a persistent pipe dream) the entry of Turkey into the war on the allied side. Churchill was dismayed. He remarked later:

> When I was at Teheran I realized for the first time what a very *small* country this is. On one hand the big Russian bear with its paws outstretched—on the other the great American Elephant—& between them the poor

> little English donkey—who is the only one that knows the right way home. (*Champion Redoubtable*, 313)

Henceforth Britain was the junior partner in the Anglo-American alliance, and Churchill a subordinate whose advice was frequently overridden. Churchill has been criticized for his 'appeasement' of the United States but, according to Brooke, he:

> hated having to give up the position of dominant partner which we had held at the start. As a result he became inclined at times to put up strategic proposals which he knew were unsound merely to spite the Americans... There lay in the back of his mind the desire to form a purely British theatre where the laurels would be all ours. (Alanbrooke, 473)

In October 1943, with the encouragement of his old friend Jan Christiaan Smuts, the prime minister of South Africa, Churchill came close to abandoning his commitment to a cross-Channel invasion. In the event it was only a brief flirtation with strategic independence after which he swallowed his pride and reverted to the principle that no dispute with the United States should ever be pushed to the point where it would imperil the alliance. One of his greatest strengths as a war leader was his ability to focus on the main priorities to the exclusion of almost everything else. In January 1944 he established a committee, over which he presided with his customary energy and vigilance, to finalize the technical preparations for Overlord, but his doubts and fears persisted almost to the last minute.

100 The most vexatious of Churchill's allies was de Gaulle. Churchill admired his haughty demeanour and prickly nationalism whenever disputes arose between the British and the Free French. But the differences between Churchill and de Gaulle were serious. Churchill hoped to detach elements of Vichy France and win them over to the allied side. De Gaulle, on the other hand, would tolerate no rivals for the leadership of France. Given the fact that de Gaulle was almost wholly dependent on British support, Churchill found his pretensions extremely tiresome. Since Roosevelt harboured an almost paranoid hostility to de Gaulle, tensions mounted after the United States entered the war. Under pressure from Roosevelt, Churchill came very close in 1943 to breaking with de Gaulle altogether, but was restrained by Eden and the cabinet. Relations were temporarily improved after the liberation when Churchill was invited to Paris. On 11 November 1944, amid the cheers of half a million people, Churchill and de Gaulle walked in a triumphant procession down the avenue des Champs-Elysées. In spite of their quarrels the two possessed a shared goal: the restoration of France as a European power.

So great was Churchill's desire to be at the scene of the action that he scarcely stopped travelling. With the formation of the grand alliance he became a globe-trotter undertaking long and hazardous journeys as though they were a matter of routine. In November 1943 Captain Pim, who was in charge of the prime minister's map room, calculated that since the outbreak of war he had travelled 110,000 miles by ship or plane. For a man in his late sixties his energy and stamina were astonishing, but the gruelling schedule and constant burden of responsibility began to take their toll.

During his first visit to Washington, in December 1941, he suffered a minor heart attack. At Tunis, in December 1943, he collapsed with a severe bout of pneumonia which put him out of action for nearly a month. Though he rallied and returned to work he was a leader on the brink of exhaustion for the rest of the war.

After the allied invasion of Normandy in June 1944, Churchill's influence over grand strategy continued to decline, and he was incensed when four French and three American divisions were diverted from the Italian campaign for landings in the Riviera (Anvil) in August 1944. Churchill also blamed the Americans for the frustration of his strategic ambitions in the Far East, where British and Commonwealth forces were tied up in Burma at the expense of operations to recapture Singapore. 'Thus two-thirds of our forces are being mis-employed for American convenience', Churchill wrote to his wife in August 1944 (Soames, 501). In September, after a therapeutic visit to Alexander's army in Italy, Churchill crossed the Atlantic on the *Queen Mary* for another meeting with Roosevelt at Quebec. There he was presented by the US treasury secretary, Henry Morgenthau, with a plan for the de-industrialization of Germany which conflicted with his own belief that a prosperous Germany was essential to the future prosperity of Europe. Although Churchill was briefly attracted to the plan, he soon changed his mind and was much relieved when it was rejected by officials on both sides of the Atlantic.

It is easy to exaggerate the consistency of Churchill's views about Soviet expansionism. In the case of Yugoslavia he decided to support the communist partisans, led by Tito, at the expense of the right-wing Chetniks, led by Mihailovic. He oscillated between phases of deep anxiety about Soviet intentions, and moments of optimism when he believed that he could establish a good working relationship with Stalin. When Churchill paid his second visit to Moscow in October 1944 he wrote out on a single sheet of paper a proposal for the division of the Balkan countries into spheres of influence expressed in percentages. Romania, for example, was to be 90 per cent in the Russian sphere and 10 per cent in the British; Greece 90 per cent British and 10 per cent Russian. Stalin read the paper, put a large tick on it, and handed it back. With the Red Army advancing into Poland, there was clearly a danger that Stalin would set up a puppet government in Warsaw. Churchill worked hard to secure a compromise that would ensure the independence of Poland, the cause for which Britain had declared war in September 1939, while conceding Polish territory east of the Curzon line to the Soviet Union. 'I have had very nice talks with the Old Bear [Stalin]', Churchill wrote to his wife. 'I like him the more I see of him. *Now* they respect us here & I am sure they wish to work with us' (Soames, 506).

In December 1944, when Churchill ordered the suppression of the Greek left, and flew to Athens to impose his will, Stalin—unlike Roosevelt—offered no dissent or opposition. Deeply impressed, Churchill concluded that Stalin had been true to his word. When the 'big three' met for the last time at Yalta in February 1945 Stalin promised to allow free elections in Poland and to respect Polish independence. 'Poor Neville believed he could trust Hitler', Churchill told his ministers. 'He was wrong. But I don't think I'm wrong about Stalin' (*War Diary of Hugh Dalton*, 836). In the aftermath of Yalta, however, as Stalin strengthened his grip on Poland, Churchill began to have second thoughts. Fears of a Germany under communist control led him to urge Roosevelt and General Eisenhower to march on Berlin and capture it before the Russians could get there, but they rejected his advice. When Roosevelt died on 12 April 1945 Churchill decided not to attend the funeral—a sign perhaps of some coolness towards an overmighty ally, and a lost opportunity for an early meeting with the new president, Harry S. Truman.

## Home affairs: defeat at the polls

Owing to his intense concentration on the conduct of the war, and frequent absences from Britain, Churchill's contacts with home affairs were intermittent. For the most part he was content to delegate. The management of the war economy was largely in the hands of the lord president's committee, chaired successively by Chamberlain, Anderson, and Attlee, while Ernest Bevin, the minister of labour, dealt with industrial relations and the reconstruction committee under Lord Woolton took charge of post-war problems. But no prime minister can afford to ignore domestic political currents for long. The price Churchill paid for doing so was defeat in the general election of 1945.

The publication in December 1942 of the Beveridge report opened up a host of peacetime questions. The immediate consequence was a crisis in the coalition as a division of opinion arose between the Labour and Conservative parties. The war cabinet attempted to paper over the cracks and Churchill himself, in a broadcast in March 1943, sought a middle way between acceptance and rejection of the report.

But his determination to postpone any legislation until after the war left the Conservatives wide open to attack from Labour on post-war questions. In March 1944 he was startled when the government lost a vote in the House of Commons on the question of equal pay for women teachers. Determined to teach his critics a lesson, Churchill turned the question into a vote of confidence which he won by a crushing majority. This merely served to confirm the widespread popular impression that Churchill was unlikely to make a good peacetime leader.

As the end of the war in Europe approached, Churchill wavered between fighting a general election and seeking to maintain the coalition for a further period. In May 1945 he invited the Labour and the Liberal parties to continue in office until the defeat of Japan, which was not expected to occur for another eighteen months. When both parties refused, Churchill resigned and returned at the head of an interim or caretaker administration: a Conservative government with a sprinkling of 'non-party' figures. During the opening broadcast of the election campaign Churchill astonished many of his admirers by warning that a Labour government would introduce into Britain 'some form of Gestapo, no doubt humanely administered in the first instance'. Churchill had been genuinely worried during the war by the inroads of state bureaucracy into civil liberty, and was clearly influenced by F. A. Hayek's anti-totalitarian tract, *The Road to Serfdom* (1944). The claim that his own deputy prime minister would resort to Nazi methods was patently absurd but probably had little impact on the result of the general election. The new generation which voted for the first time in 1945 was predominantly Labour, shaped by the egalitarianism and left-wing propaganda of the war years.

Unusually, there was an interlude between polling day (5 July) and the declaration of the results (26 July), during which Churchill attended the Potsdam conference. Stalin—whom he was never to meet again—seems again to have persuaded him, for the moment, that his intentions were benign. After a brief holiday Churchill was back in Britain for the result of the general election, which proved to be a landslide Labour victory. 'It may well be a blessing in disguise', Clementine remarked. 'At the moment it seems quite effectively disguised', Churchill replied (Churchill, *Second World War*, 6.583). He had, however, a majority of over 17,000 in his constituency of Woodford (as it was now designated). At 7 p.m. on 26 July he drove to Buckingham Palace and resigned, declining the king's offer of the Order of the Garter.

Clementine urged Churchill to retire but he was determined to stay on. With the next general election a distant prospect, he tended to neglect his role as Conservative leader, absenting himself for long periods from the House of Commons. In foreign and defence policy the scope for opposition was limited, since he was broadly in agreement with the government's policies, but he lashed out with much hyperbole against alleged socialist mismanagement of the economy and the proliferation of controls in which he detected totalitarian tendencies. Nor did Churchill approve of the government's preparations for the transfer of power in India, which he regarded as hasty and irresponsible. He warned in March 1947:

> In handing over the Government of India to these so-called political classes, we are handing over to men of straw, of whom, in a few years, no trace will remain ... It is with deep grief I watch the clattering down of the British Empire with all its glories and all the services it has rendered to mankind. (Churchill, *Europe Unite*, 21, 25)

Churchill nevertheless had to accept that it was too late to put the clock back, and finally gave his support to the Independence of India Bill.

Due to his lavish spending habits, Churchill had never amassed great wealth. But in 1946 a consortium of wealthy benefactors, led by Lord Camrose, purchased Chartwell and presented it to the National Trust, on condition that he and Clementine would have the right to live there for the rest of their lives. In order to avoid penal rates of income tax on the prodigious sums Churchill could now command as an author, he gave his papers to the Chartwell Trust, which then sold the literary rights, employed the tax-free income generated for the benefit of his children and grandchildren, and paid him £20,000 a year—double the prime minister's salary—for living and research expenses. In his book *In Command of History*, one of the great landmarks in Churchill scholarship, David Reynolds calculated that the literary rights to *The Second World War* were sold for a figure worth somewhere between eighteen million and sixty million dollars in today's money (Reynolds, 62).

In order to write *The Second World War* Churchill assembled a team of researchers, known as 'the Syndicate' under the leadership of his pre-war assistant, the Oxford historian

William Deakin. Churchill and his team enjoyed the full co-operation of the cabinet secretary, Norman Brook, who gave them almost unlimited access to wartime files. In return Churchill submitted drafts of the book to be vetted by Whitehall, thus turning it into a semi-official history. His method was to have all the relevant documents set up in galley proof so that he could then insert linking passages or narratives of events. The tone and structure of the final text were unmistakably Churchillian, and so too were his personal recollections, but it would have come as a great surprise to readers at the time to learn that a number of the key passages, like the account of the rise of Hitler or the evacuation from Dunkirk, were ghost written. There were even a few pages written by Norman Brook himself.

Appearing in six volumes between 1948 and 1954, *The Second World War* was published in hardback in fifteen countries and translated into eleven languages. It was not history, Churchill insisted, but a contribution to history. Nevertheless he imprinted his version of events on the minds of a generation. He savaged the policies of appeasement and argued that the Second World War could have been prevented by timely action against Hitler. Perhaps for reasons of national prestige, he suppressed all reference to the war cabinet's discussion of compromise peace in May 1940. Writing in the context of the cold war, he played down or suppressed evidence of Anglo-American differences, and contrived, with some sleight of hand, to refute American critics who claimed that he had tried to avoid a cross-Channel invasion of Europe. There was no mention of Ultra, which remained a closely guarded secret until the 1970s, and barely a hint of his disputes with the chiefs of staff.

# The post-war world

# 10

## Iron curtain and European union

Churchill's interpretation of the Second World War was one of a triptych of themes he developed between 1945 and 1951: the second was the Soviet danger and the third the case for European unity. Towards the end of 1945 Churchill received an invitation to give one in a series of annual lectures at Fulton College in Missouri. There, on 5 March 1946, he gave the first public warning by a leading British or American statesman of the impending struggle between the West and the Soviet Union. 'From Stettin in the Baltic to Trieste in the Adriatic', he declared, 'an iron curtain has descended across the Continent' (Churchill and Gilbert, 8.200). Delivered at a time when there was still much goodwill towards Russia as a wartime ally, Churchill's 'iron curtain' speech provoked much hostile comment in the United States and western Europe. But it was in harmony with the views of many insiders in Washington and Whitehall. Truman himself, though feigning ignorance of its contents, had read and endorsed the speech in advance. Subsequently, as relations between the West and the Soviet Union deteriorated,

Churchill's views achieved wide acceptance, and his Fulton speech was hailed as prophetic. By this time, however, Churchill was privately urging that Britain and the United States should exploit their temporary nuclear monopoly to deliver an ultimatum to the Soviet Union: if it was rejected, the atom bomb would be dropped on Russia. The news of a successful Soviet atomic test in August 1949 seems to have put an end to these reckless imaginings.

In September 1946 Churchill made his second great contribution to the post-war world in a speech at the University of Zürich. As at Fulton, he was attempting to detach his audience from wartime emotions and prepare them for a new post-war reality. He called for the reconciliation of France and Germany and the establishment of a united Europe in which the sovereignty of nation states was pooled for the common good. Evidently his call for the unification of Europe owed something to the cold war context, but it was a concept he had first formulated in 1930, and reverted to between 1940 and 1945. So great was Churchill's stature that his speeches gave a powerful impetus to the movement for a united Europe and he came to be regarded as one of its founding fathers. Churchill also accepted the leadership of the British European movement and criticized the Labour government for failing to play a more constructive role in the formation of European unity. In June 1950 he attacked the government for refusing to participate in the conference called to implement the Schuman plan for a European iron and steel community. In August, at the opening session of the consultative assembly of the Council of Europe at Strasbourg, he successfully moved a resolution in favour of the creation of a European army and appeared to suggest that

Britain would play a part in it. All this led some observers to conclude that Churchill was a committed European. But as he explained in a speech to the Conservative Party conference (9 October 1948), Churchill believed that Britain had a unique role to play as the link between 'the three great circles among the free nations and democracies'—Britain and the empire, the United States, and a united Europe (Parker, *Statesmanship*, 201).

In the post-war years honours and hospitality were showered upon Churchill. He was awarded the freedom of several European cities, together with medals and honorary doctorates. While the British endured rationing, austerity, and restrictions on overseas travel, villas and châteaux in the sun were at his disposal, and few begrudged him the fruits of victory. His marriage to Clemmie remained the cornerstone of his private life, though his oldest friend and companion, his younger brother Jack, died in 1947. Churchill took up painting again, exhibiting at the Royal Academy, and suddenly acquired an enthusiasm for one of his father's recreations, the turf. He was the owner, at various times, of some thirty-seven racehorses, including a French stallion, Colonist II, who won thirteen races in Lord Randolph's colours before he was put to stud. When asked if Colonist was still racing he replied: 'No, he has given up racing. He is now rogering' (Montague Browne, 151).

In January 1950 Attlee called a general election. Churchill took a less prominent part in the campaign than in 1945, and his attacks on socialism were balanced by a more conciliatory tone in home affairs. He also called, in a speech in Edinburgh, for a summit meeting between the leaders of the great powers—the first indication of a new approach to the Soviet Union. The Labour government, however, was returned to power with a precarious majority of six, and managed to struggle on until autumn 1951. Churchill strongly supported the government over the Korean War, which broke out in June 1950, but attacked them vigorously for their alleged weakness in Iran, where a revolutionary regime under Dr Mussadiq nationalized the Anglo-Iranian oil company. (As prime minister Churchill was later to be a party to the Anglo-American-inspired coup which led to the overthrow of Mussadiq in 1953.)

## Prime minister in peacetime

When another general election was called in October 1951, Churchill again floated the idea of a 'conference at the summit'. He was strongly attacked from the Labour side as a warmonger and on polling day the *Daily Mirror* carried on its front page a large picture of a revolver and the question: 'Whose finger? Today YOUR finger is on the trigger.' This time, however, Labour was defeated and the Conservatives restored to power with a majority of seventeen.

Returning to 10 Downing Street (26 October 1951) at nearly seventy-seven years of age, Churchill formed a government with many echoes of his wartime premiership. He even resumed the title of minister of defence, though after a few months he persuaded a reluctant Field Marshal Alexander to accept the post. Anthony Eden returned in the role of foreign secretary, crown prince, and long-suffering subordinate. General Ismay and Viscount Cherwell were both given cabinet posts, and John Colville was recalled as his private secretary. Churchill attempted to create a coalition by inviting the Liberal leader, Clement Davies, to be minister of education, but the offer was declined. In home affairs the appointments of R. A. Butler as chancellor of the exchequer, Walter Monckton as minister of labour, and Harold Macmillan as minister of housing, signalled a relatively moderate approach. In a curious experiment, Churchill began by appointing a number of peers, including Leathers and Woolton, as 'overlords' to co-ordinate the policies of groups of departments. The overlords, however, having no departments to sustain them in the battles of Whitehall, quickly faded away.

At the death of George VI on 6 February 1952, Churchill broadcast a graceful tribute over the radio. He was deeply moved by the king's death and the succession of Elizabeth II, from whom he accepted the Order of the Garter in April 1953. The coronation (2 June 1953) was the last great pageant of an empire whose decline was masked, for the time being, by the charismatic conjunction of the aged statesman and the beautiful young queen.

By now Churchill was no longer a dynamic force. A fresh supply of 'action this day' stickers was printed, but this time they were left unused. As he was going deaf, he had to be supplied with a hearing aid for cabinet meetings. With much guidance from the cabinet secretary, Norman Brook, he chaired the cabinet in his usual discursive style until June 1953, when he suffered a stroke which left him partially paralysed. The nature of his illness was concealed by a secret circle of conspirators, led by R. A. Butler and Lord Salisbury, who doctored the medical bulletin and persuaded the press to collude in the fiction that Churchill was merely taking a rest. His son-in-law, Christopher Soames, took over the running of 10 Downing Street in the interim. At first Churchill thought he was finished but within a few days he began to recover and by the autumn he was well enough to return to work. On great occasions, like his speech to the Conservative Party conference at Blackpool in October, he could still put on a dazzling performance, but the remainder of his political life hung by a thread.

The first few months of Churchill's peacetime government were overshadowed by economic crisis, a fresh round of austerity, and a great debate in Whitehall over whether or not to adopt the radical course of floating the pound (operation Robot). These were matters in which Churchill was out of his depth, though not without a politician's instinct for survival. The programme of the tory party, he explained late one night at Chequers, must be 'houses and meat and not being scuppered' (Colville, *Fringes of Power*, 644). Largely on the advice of Cherwell, he decided against Robot. Generally speaking Churchill was bored by home affairs, but he rejoiced in the abolition of food rationing, and welcomed the decision to end the BBC's monopoly of television. Simultaneously he gave strong support to Harold Macmillan's housing programme against opposition from the Treasury. Determined to avoid industrial strife he instructed his minister of labour, Walter Monckton, to pursue a policy of appeasing the trade unions at the cost, if necessary, of inflationary wage settlements. On racial questions, Churchill was still a late Victorian. He tried in vain to manoeuvre the cabinet into restricting West Indian immigration. 'Keep England White' was a good slogan, he told the cabinet in January 1955 (Hennessy, 205).

Churchill sought a quiet life at home in order to concentrate on his main objective, the restoration of Britain as a great power. Once in office, he displayed no more enthusiasm than the Labour government for British involvement in the Schuman plan and his support for the creation of a European army (which he privately referred to as a 'sludgy amalgam') did not extend to British participation. But he threw himself into a passionate last-ditch defence of Britain's military base in the Suez Canal zone against the demands of Egyptian leaders for a British withdrawal. 'He never wavered', wrote Roger Louis, 'from his Victorian opinion that the Egyptians were an inferior and essentially cowardly people' (Blake and Louis, 473). This was an issue on which Churchill was frequently at odds with his foreign secretary, Anthony Eden, whose attempts to reach a settlement with Egypt he stigmatized as appeasement. By 1954, however, Churchill was compelled to recognize that his views commanded little support. Consoling himself with the argument that the Suez base was strategically obsolete in a nuclear age, he accepted the inevitable.

Churchill's first priority when he returned to power was the re-establishment of the Anglo-American 'special relationship'. In January 1952 he crossed the Atlantic in the *Queen Mary* for discussions with President Truman. Outwardly relations were full of bonhomie, but the president and his advisers did not share Churchill's conception of an Anglo-American global alliance. They rejected his pleas for American military support in the Suez Canal zone and made few concessions to his request for the restoration of the Quebec agreement on the use of nuclear weapons. When Eisenhower was elected president in November 1952, Churchill hastened to Washington for consultations with his former wartime comrade-in-arms. But greatly though Eisenhower liked and admired Churchill, he thought his view of Anglo-American relations sentimental and privately concluded that he was living in the wartime past. Churchill's pleas for diplomatic support over Egypt were rejected. Nor did 'Ike' warm to Churchill's idea of a summit conference with the Russians. Even more discouraging was the new secretary of state, John Foster Dulles, a doctrinaire anti-communist for whom Churchill developed a strong antipathy.

Although Churchill pressed repeatedly for discussions with the Kremlin, he never defined the terms of the settlement he was seeking, and his motives appear to have been mixed. Surrounded by whispers that he was unfit for office, and under constant pressure to make way for Eden, he badly needed a justification for clinging to power, and also, perhaps, relished the prospect of outmanoeuvring the Labour Party. Whatever his motives, there is no doubt that his last great ambition was to play the role of peacemaker. With the death of Stalin on 5 March 1953 his hopes of *détente* rose, but his attempts to seize the initiative were interrupted by illness. In December 1953 Eisenhower attended a conference in Bermuda at Churchill's invitation, but again rejected his proposals for a common approach to Russia. When Churchill flew to Washington in June 1954 he was surprised and elated when Eisenhower withdrew his objections and even agreed that Churchill should go alone to Moscow. During the return voyage on the *Queen Elizabeth* Churchill in cavalier fashion dispatched a telegram to the Soviet foreign minister Molotov without consulting the cabinet. The consequence, when he got home, was a cabinet crisis in which he was strongly opposed by Eden and other senior ministers. From this impasse the Russians, quite unwittingly, extricated him by clumsy diplomacy.

Churchill was, of course, no unilateral disarmer. It was under his chairmanship that the defence committee of the cabinet decided in June 1954 to recommend that Britain must build its hydrogen bomb as a deterrent against Soviet attack. But Churchill also grasped the fact that with both the United States and the Soviet Union in possession of nuclear weapons, the world now stood on the brink of self-destruction. His last major speech in the House of Commons (1 March 1955) was devoted to the dangers of nuclear holocaust but ended on a note of hope: 'It may well be that we shall, by a process of sublime irony, have reached a stage where safety will be the sturdy shield of terror, and survival the twin brother of annihilation' (Churchill and Gilbert, 8.1100).

## Resignation and retirement

In November 1954 Churchill celebrated his eightieth birthday. Presented by parliament with an official portrait by Graham Sutherland, he declared that it was 'a remarkable example of modern art', but was deeply wounded by the artist's presentation of him as an old man battling against physical decay. The painting was later burnt by Clementine. Even Churchill, however, had to accept that he was too old to lead the Conservatives into another general election. On 5 April 1955, after entertaining the queen and the duke of Edinburgh to dinner at 10 Downing Street, he tendered his resignation. The queen offered him a dukedom but

Churchill remained an MP until 1964, sometimes voting in parliamentary divisions, but never again speaking in the house. At the height of the Suez crisis in October 1956 Eden contacted Churchill's private secretary, Anthony Montague Browne, to ask whether Churchill would accept a seat in the cabinet. Montague Browne took it upon himself to decline on his master's behalf. Churchill's private verdict on the Suez fiasco was telling: 'I would never have done it without squaring the Americans, and once I'd started I'd never have dared stop' (Montague Browne, 213). When Eden resigned, Churchill was among those advising the queen to choose Harold Macmillan as his successor.

In his retirement Churchill set one new project on foot. Impressed by Viscount Cherwell's warnings about the lack of scientific and technological manpower in Britain, he led a financial appeal for the establishment of a British equivalent of the Massachusetts Institute of Technology. The outcome, though less ambitious than Churchill intended, was a new Cambridge college named after him and devoted to science and technology. Churchill also returned to the task of revising his *History of the English-Speaking Peoples*. Published in four volumes in 1956 and 1957, it was received with widespread acclaim, but of all his major works it was the least successful in standing the test of time. That it should take the form of a narrative of kings, battles, and constitutional landmarks, with social and economic history relegated to the margins, was only to be expected. The real problem was that it lacked the true Churchillian fire of passionate engagement with the subject. Most of the book read like a carefully polished synthesis of the drafts prepared for him by academic historians. Churchill had originally intended that it would demonstrate the shared heritage and destiny of Britain and the United States, but this was a theme he failed to dramatize or develop.

As Churchill's mental and physical faculties decayed, he began to lose the battle he had fought for so long against the 'black dog' of depression. He found some solace in the sunshine and colours of the Mediterranean. He took long holidays with his literary adviser Emery Reves and his wife, Wendy Russell, at La Pausa, their villa on the French Riviera. Clementine, who was often herself in poor health and did not approve of Winston's growing affection for Wendy, seldom joined him on these excursions. He also took eight cruises aboard the yacht *Christina* as the guest of the Greek shipowner Aristotle Onassis. Once, when the *Christina* had to pass through the Dardanelles, Onassis gave instructions that it was to do so during the night, so as not to disturb his guest with unhappy memories.

# 11 'Remember Winston Churchill'

## Qualities and flaws

Churchill's final years were melancholy. He approved the appointment of Randolph as his official biographer, but the love–hate relationship between father and son was never resolved. Sarah was descending into alcoholism and Diana committed suicide in the autumn of 1964. Churchill himself suffered a number of minor strokes. It was a figure ravaged by age and sorrow who appeared at the window of his London home, 28 Hyde Park Gate, to greet the photographers on his ninetieth birthday in November 1964. In December he dined for the last time at the Other Club, sitting in silence but apparently knowing where he was. On 10 January he suffered another stroke and after lingering for a fortnight died at 28 Hyde Park Gate shortly after eight o'clock on the morning of Sunday 24 January 1965, seventy years to the day after the death of Lord Randolph.

On the instructions of the queen, a state funeral had been long planned by officials under the code name operation Hope-Not. After lying in state for three days in Westminster

Hall the coffin, covered in a union flag, was taken in procession to St Paul's Cathedral for the funeral service, then embarked at Tower Pier on a Port of London launch. As the launch passed up river, the quayside cranes were dipped in salute. From Waterloo station the coffin travelled slowly by train to Bladon. In the fields along the route, and at the stations through which the train passed, thousands stood in silence to pay their last respects. In the village churchyard at Bladon, where his mother and father and his brother Jack were buried, his body was interred in a private family ceremony.

In September 1965 the queen unveiled a memorial stone set in the floor of Westminster Abbey and inscribed: 'Remember Winston Churchill'. At the time it seemed unthinkable that anyone could forget. He was not only a British hero, but a hero of western Europe and the English-speaking world. At the beginning of the twenty-first century some of that fame endures, but young people know little of him, and shifting historical perspectives have made the task of assessing him more complex. Churchill's war leadership, together with his writings and speeches, persuaded a generation to accept his version of history and the part he had played in it. In his own estimate he was a prophet, a strategist of deep insight, and a statesman of strong and consistent convictions. But this version of the past was at odds with the experience of many of the people with whom he had worked, not to mention those who had fought or opposed him. Among his contemporaries, only the most narrow-minded denied him great qualities: volcanic energy, physical and mental courage, eloquence and vision, humanity and wit. Almost all conceded that he possessed elements of genius. But he was, they concluded, a genius *manqué* whose more brilliant qualities were offset by serious flaws: supreme egotism, an adventurer's love of daring but perilous courses of action, poor judgement of men, erratic changes of course, susceptibility to rhetoric and flights of the imagination. Brooke mused in August 1943:

> I wonder whether any historian of the future will ever be able to paint Winston in his true colours. It is a wonderful character—the most marvellous qualities and superhuman genius mixed with an astonishing lack of vision at times, and an impetuosity which if not guided must inevitably bring him into trouble again and again. (Alanbrooke, 451)

Churchill's death was followed by a flurry of revisionism in which the doubts and criticisms, buried for a quarter of a century beneath the wartime legend, were rediscovered. In the works of Robert Rhodes James, Lord Moran, and others, Churchill was depicted warts and all, with a focus on errors of judgement and foibles of character. But revisionism proved to be a two-way street. The official biography of Churchill, begun by Randolph Churchill and carried to a triumphant conclusion by the prodigious labours of Martin Gilbert, was an exhaustive, day-by-day chronicle without an analytical framework. But it also set the record straight. Many of the more facile allegations against Churchill 'the warmonger' were shown to be untrue, and a more rounded portrait created through an emphasis on his more peaceful and constructive endeavours.

The completion of the official biography was followed by a second wave of revisionism, more radical than the first.

 Churchill was accused of racism, militarism, and sympathy with fascism. Hitherto acclaimed as the saviour of his country, he was now accused of leading Britain into a war that fatally undermined its power and prestige. His faith in the special relationship between Britain and the United States was interpreted as a dangerous illusion and the outcome of the war as a self-inflicted defeat. As John Charmley put it:

> Churchill stood for the British Empire, for British independence and for an 'anti-Socialist' vision of Britain. By July 1945 the first of these was on the skids, the second was dependent solely on America, and the third had just vanished in a Labour election victory. It was indeed the end of glory. (Charmley, *End of Glory*, 649)

Iconoclasm attracted much attention but was no more persuasive than the hagiography it sought to replace. There is no reason to doubt the essential truth of the portrait of Churchill painted by those who knew him best. His unexpected emergence as a national hero in 1940 was the consequence of an exceptional moment in British history that transformed even his flaws into virtues: suddenly his egotism, bellicosity, imperious demands, high-flown rhetoric, romantic vision, and cavalier indifference to party were rare and precious assets, while the elements of genius which had been evident for so long shone far more brightly than ever. All his adult life Churchill had been a master of the English language: now it fell to him to express the general will. As he said himself, on his eightieth birthday: 'It was the nation and the race dwelling all round the globe that had the lion's heart. I had the luck to be called upon to give the roar' (Churchill and Gilbert, 8.1075).

For Churchill himself the Second World War was both 'triumph and tragedy'—the title he gave to the sixth and final volume of his book. The triumph lay in the defeat of Nazi Germany, the preservation of British institutions, and the restoration of parliamentary democracy in western Europe. The tragedy lay in the decline of the empire, the advance of Soviet communism into eastern Europe, and the failure of the Anglo-American relationship to live up to Churchill's expectations. In the last years of his life, oppressed by physical decay and the black dog of depression, he began to think that his life's work had come to nothing. There is no need to accept this verdict. Whatever the price the British paid for victory in the Second World War, the cost of defeat would have been much greater. In all essentials Churchill was right about the rise of Hitler's Germany, the need for rearmament and collective security, and the necessity of waging war. Without him the whole of Europe, Britain included, might have experienced decades of Nazi rule.

## Honours and images

In the course of a lifetime Churchill was the recipient of thirty-seven orders, decorations, and medals. He was made a Companion of Honour in 1922, awarded the Order of Merit in 1946, and the Order of the Garter in 1953. After stepping down as prime minister Churchill refused the offer of a dukedom, though he was tempted for a while by the prospect of becoming duke of London. His medals included the Spanish cross of the order of military merit (1895), the India medal with clasp, Punjab Frontier 1897–8 (1898), the Queen's Sudan medal, 1896–8 (1899), and the Queen's South Africa medal, 1899–1902, with six clasps (1901). After the

 Second World War he was awarded high honours by Belgium, Luxemburg, the Netherlands, Norway, Denmark, and France.

Churchill was sworn of the privy council in 1907, was created lord warden of the Cinque Ports in 1941, and was made a fellow of the Royal Society the same year. He was rector of the universities of Aberdeen (1914–18) and Edinburgh (1929–32), and chancellor of the University of Bristol (1930). He received honorary doctorates in law from Rochester and Harvard universities in the United States, and McGill University in Canada, and an honorary doctorate in philosophy from the University of Copenhagen. In 1953 he was awarded the Nobel prize for literature 'for his mastery of historical and biographical description as well as for brilliant oratory in defending exalted human values.' On the initiative of President John F. Kennedy, the two houses of the United States congress passed in 1963 a resolution making him an honorary citizen of the United States. In April 1999 he became the first Briton to have a United States warship named after him: the USS *Winston S. Churchill*, a guided missile destroyer.

The earliest known portrait of Churchill, as a boy aged four in Dublin, is by Cyron Ward (1878). Of the many later portraits the most notable are perhaps those by Sir William Orpen (1915) and Sir John Lavery (1916), depicting a sombre and troubled Churchill at the nadir of his fortunes. The most memorable portraits of Churchill in the Second World War were the work of photographers including Cecil Beaton (1940), showing him at work in the cabinet room, and Karsh of Ottawa (1941), who claimed to have captured Churchill's bulldog expression in one of the photographs by snatching the cigar from his mouth. There is, of course, a wealth of press photographs in the picture libraries, and the newsreel archives contain hundreds of Churchill sequences. Among the cartoonists, the New Zealander David Low was pre-eminent in portraying Churchill over a period of more than three decades in a sequence of caricatures from a left-wing perspective. Equally famous in his day was Sidney Strube, staff cartoonist for the *Daily Express* from 1912 to 1948. It was he who first drew the head of Churchill on the body of a bulldog (8 June 1940) thus creating the classic wartime image. 'Vicky' (Victor Weisz) produced one of the wittiest of all commentaries on the many facets of Churchill with his depiction of the different styles in which his portrait might have been painted by artists from Holbein to Picasso. In addition to the bronze head of Churchill by Jacob Epstein (1946), there are statues of Churchill by David McFall at Woodford (1959), William McVey outside the British embassy in Washington (1966), Franta Belsky at Fulton, Missouri (1969), Oscar Nemon in the House of Commons (1969), and Jean Cardot in Paris (1998). In Ivor Roberts-Jones's statue in Parliament Square (1976) Churchill appears as a hunched and brooding giant, stalking defiantly into a menacing future.

Churchill was also commemorated in ephemera which date back to the earliest years of his fame. He first appeared on a piece of commemorative china—a teapot—in 1900. Cigarette cards recorded his escape from Boer prisoner of war camp and postcards his wedding to Clementine. As first lord of the Admiralty during the First World War he appeared on scarves, handkerchieves, and ceramics. The first-ever Churchill toby jug featured him as chancellor of the exchequer in 1927, the forerunner of a spate of toby jugs, bronze bulldogs, tea plates, and other patriotic memorabilia which flooded onto the market between 1939 and 1945. The iconography of Churchill owed much to his awareness of the importance of imagery in politics and his image was no less important in establishing his fame than his speeches.

Churchill sometimes blundered, but his giant stature does not rest on the claim that he was always right. Right or wrong, he was an exceptionally great man by virtue of the extraordinary range of qualities he possessed. In his obituary of Churchill the Labour politician Michael Foot accused him of numerous failings and follies. But he also wrote:

> Seen from any angle, the scale of the figure on the vast canvas is stupendous. Not merely does Churchill bestride the century; not merely has he been a foremost performer in British and world politics for a longer period than almost any rival in ancient or modern times. The same giant lineaments are revealed when his particular faculties are examined. His vitality, his brainpower, his endurance, his wit, his eloquence, his industry, his application were superabundant, superhuman ... the man was huge. (Foot, 168)

# Sources

R. S. Churchill and M. Gilbert, *Winston S. Churchill*, 8 vols. (1966–88) · R. S. Churchill and M. Gilbert, eds., *Winston S. Churchill: companion*, 5 vols. (1967–79) · M. Gilbert, ed., *The Churchill war papers*, 3 vols. (1993–9) · W. S. Churchill, *The story of the Malakand field force* (1898), repr. (1989) · W. S. Churchill, *The river war*, 2 vols. (1899); 1 vol. (1973) · W. S. Churchill, *Savrola* (1957) · W. S. Churchill, *Lord Randolph Churchill* (1950) · W. S. Churchill, *My African journey* (1972) · W. S. Churchill, *The people's rights* (1970) · W. S. Churchill, *The world crisis*, 5 vols. (1923–9) · W. S. Churchill, *My early life* (1930) · W. S. Churchill, *Thoughts and adventures* (1932) · W. S. Churchill, *Marlborough: his life and times*, 4 vols. (1933–8) · W. S. Churchill, *Great contemporaries* (1937) · W. S. Churchill, *The Second World War*, 6 vols. (1948–54) · W. S. Churchill, *A history of the English-speaking peoples*, 4 vols. (1956–8) · W. S. Churchill, *Europe unite: speeches 1947 and 1948*, ed. R. S. Churchill (1950) · W. S. Churchill, *Secret session speeches* (1946) · *Winston S. Churchill: his complete speeches*, ed. R. Rhodes James, 8 vols. (1974) · W. F. Kimball, ed., *Churchill and Roosevelt: the complete correspondence*, 3 vols. (1984) · M. Soames, ed., *Speaking for themselves: the personal letters of Winston and Clementine Churchill* (1998) · *The collected essays of Sir Winston Churchill*, ed. M. Wolff, 3 vols. [n.d.] · F. Woods, ed., *Young Winston's wars* (1972) · Lord Alanbrooke, *War diaries, 1939–1945*, ed. A. Danchev and D. Todman (2001) · J. B. Atkins, *Incidents and reflections* (1947) · H. Begbie,

*The mirrors of Downing Street* (1920) · V. Bonham-Carter, *Winston Churchill as I knew him* (1965) · Lord Bridges, 'Working with Churchill', *Winston Churchill: tributes broadcast by the BBC* (1965), 95–7 · A. Montague Browne, *Long sunset* (1995) · R. S. Churchill, *Twenty-one years* (1965) · *Churchill by his contemporaries: an 'Observer' appreciation* (1965) · J. Colville, *Footprints in time: memories* (1976) · J. Colville, *The fringes of power: Downing Street diaries, 1939–1955* (1985) · *The diaries of Sir Alexander Cadogan, 1938–1945*, ed. D. Dilks (1971) · M. Foot, *Loyalists and loners* (1986) · A. G. Gardiner, *Prophets, priests and kings* (1914) · A. D. Gibb, *With Winston Churchill at the front* (1924) · H. L. Ismay, *Memoirs* (1960) · T. Jones, *Whitehall diary*, ed. K. Middlemas, 3 vols. (1969–71) · *The Riddell diaries, 1908–1923*, ed. J. M. McEwen (1986) · *The diary of Beatrice Webb*, ed. N. MacKenzie and J. MacKenzie, 4 vols. (1982–5), vol. 2 · G. Mallaby, *From my level* (1965) · A. J. Marder, *From the Dreadnought to Scapa Flow: the Royal Navy in the Fisher era, 1904–1919*, 5 vols. (1961–70), vol. 1 · Lord Moran, *Winston Churchill: the struggle for survival, 1940–1965* (1966) · *The Second World War diary of Hugh Dalton, 1940–1945*, ed. B. Pimlott (1986) · *Champion redoubtable: the diaries and letters of Violet Bonham-Carter, 1914–1945*, ed. M. Pottle (1999) · *Memoirs of a Conservative: J. C. C. Davidson's memoirs and papers, 1910–37*, ed. R. R. James (1969) · G. Riddell, *More pages from my diary, 1908–1914* (1934) · P. Addison, *Churchill on the home front, 1900–1955* (1992) · P. Addison, *Churchill: The unexpected hero* (2005) · T. Ben Moshe, *Churchill as historian and strategist* (1992) · G. Bennett, *Churchill's man of mystery: Desmond Morton and the world of intelligence* (2006) · G. Best, *Churchill: a study in greatness* (2000) · G. Best, *Churchill and war* (2005) · R. Blake and W. R. Louis, eds., *Churchill* (1993) · M. C. Bromage, *Churchill and Ireland* (1964) · D. Cannadine, 'Churchill and the British monarchy', *Transactions* of *the Royal Historical Society*, 6th ser., 11 (2001), 249–72 · D. Carlton, *Churchill and the Soviet Union* (2000) · J. Charmley, *Churchill: the end of glory* (1993) · J. Charmley, *Churchill's grand alliance: the Anglo-American special relationship, 1940–1957* (1995) · M. J. Cohen, *Churchill and the Jews* (1985) · M. Gilbert, *Churchill: a life* (1991) · P. Gretton, *Former naval person: Winston Churchill and the Royal Navy* (1968) · D. Hall, 'Bulldog Churchill: the evolution of a famous image', *Finest Hour*, 106 (2000), 18–20 · D. Hall, *The book of Churchilliana* (2002) · P. Hennessy, *Prime minister: the office and its holders since 1945* (2001) · R. Hyam, *Churchill and Elgin at the colonial office* (1968) · R. Jenkins, *Churchill* (2000) · F. Kersaudy, *Churchill and de Gaulle* (1981) · W. Kimball, *Forged in war: Churchill, Roosevelt and the Second World War* (1997) · S. Lawlor, *Churchill and the politics of war, 1940–1941* (1994) · R. Lewin, *Churchill as warlord* (1973) · A. Marder, 'Winston is back: Churchill at the admiralty, 1939–1940', *English Historical Review*, suppl. 5 (1972) · J. H. Mather, 'Lord Randolph Churchill: maladies et mort', *Finest Hour*, 93 (1996–7), 23–8 · J. W. Muller, ed., *Churchill as peacemaker* (1997) · J. W. Muller, ed., *Churchill's 'iron curtain' speech fifty years later* (1999) · R. A. C. Parker, ed., *Winston Churchill: studies in statesmanship* (1995) · R. A. C. Parker, *Churchill and appeasement* (2000) · H. Pelling, *Winston Churchill* (1974) · R. Quinault, 'Churchill and democracy', *Transactions* of *the Royal Historical Society*, 6th ser., 11 (2001), 201–20 · J. Ramsden, *The age of Churchill and Eden, 1940–1957* (1995) · E. L. Rasor, *Winston S. Churchill, 1874–1965: a comprehensive historiography and annotated bibliography* (2000) · D. Reynolds, 'Churchill's writing of history: appeasement, autobiography and *The gathering storm*', *Transactions* of *the Royal Historical Society*, 6th ser., 11 (2001), 221–48 · D. Reynolds, *In command of history: Churchill fighting and writing the Second World War* (2004) · R. Rhodes James, *Churchill: a study in failure, 1900–1939* (1973) · A. Roberts, *Eminent Churchillians* (1994) · N. Rose, *Churchill: an unruly life* (1994) · S. Roskill, *Churchill and the admirals* (1977) · A. Seldon, *Churchill's Indian summer: the conservative government, 1951–55* (1981) · D. S. Russell, *Winston Churchill soldier: the military life of a gentleman at war* (2005) · D. Stafford, *Churchill and secret service* (1997) · G. Stewart, *Burying Caesar: Churchill, Chamberlain and the battle for the tory party* (1999) · *Sunday Times* (13 July 1980) · A. J. P. Taylor and others, *Churchill: four faces and the man* (1969) · C. Thorne, *Allies of a kind: the United States, Britain and the war against Japan, 1941–1945* (1978) · D. C. Watt, 'Churchill and appeasement' in *Churchill*, ed. R. Blake and W. R. Louis (1993),199-214 · E. T. Williams, 'Churchill, Sir Winston Leonard Spencer', *Dictionary of National Biography* (1981) · T. Wilson, *Churchill and the prof*

(1995) · I. S. Wood, *Churchill* (2000) · C. Wrigley, 'Churchill and the trade unions', *Transactions* of *the Royal Historical Society*, 6th ser., 11 (2001), 273–94 · J. Young, *Winston Churchill's last campaign: Britain and the cold war, 1951–1955* (1996) · Calendars of the grants of probate . . . made in . . . HM court of probate [England and Wales] (1965)

# Index

## S



## T



## U

## *W*